Leadership
in Human Services

Leslie H. Garner, Jr.

Leadership in Human Services

How to Articulate and Implement a Vision to Achieve Results

Developed in collaboration with
the National Child Welfare Leadership Center
School of Social Work
University of North Carolina, Chapel Hill

Jossey-Bass Publishers

San Francisco • London • 1989

LEADERSHIP IN HUMAN SERVICES
How to Articulate and Implement a Vision to Achieve Results
by Leslie H. Garner, Jr.

Copyright © 1989 by: Jossey-Bass Inc., Publishers
350 Sansome Street
San Francisco, California 94104
&
Jossey-Bass Limited
28 Banner Street
London EC1Y 8QE

A shorter version of Chapter Four appeared as "Critical Success
Factors in Human Services," *New England Journal of Human Services*,
1986, *6* (1), 27–31.
A shorter version of Chapter Eight appeared in the *Journal of State
Government*, 1987, *60* (4), 191–195.
Parts of Chapter Ten appeared as "Using Information to Shape the Policy
Agenda: New Perspectives on the Executive's Role," in *Administration
in Social Work*, 1987, *11* (1), 69–80.

Library of Congress Cataloging-in-Publication Data

Garner, Leslie H., Jr.
  Leadership in human services.

  (Jossey-Bass social and behavioral science series)
(Jossey-Bass public administration series)
  "Developed in collaboration with the National Child
Welfare Leadership Center, University of North Carolina,
Chapel Hill."
  Bibliography: p.
  Includes index.
  1. Human services—United States—Administration.
I. University of North Carolina at Chapel Hill.
National Child Welfare Leadership Center. II. Title.
III. Series. IV. Series: Jossey-Bass public administration series.
HV91.G337   1989   361'.0068   88-32074
ISBN 1-55542-144-X (alk. paper)

Manufactured in the United States of America

JACKET DESIGN BY WILLI BAUM

FIRST EDITION

Code 8917

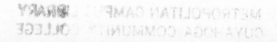

A joint publication in
The Jossey-Bass
Social and Behavioral Science Series
and
The Jossey-Bass
Public Administration Series

Contents

Preface

If you care about human services—about the problems of the disadvantaged and the need for effective solutions to these problems—this book is for you. Every day, thousands of men and women like you devote their professional time to managing the public and private agencies that deliver human services. They endure enormous frustration, but they continue because they believe in what they do. Whether you are currently a leader or a student of leadership in human services, *Leadership in Human Services* is written to help you understand how to be more effective.

You may wonder why you should read another book on leadership. There are already scores of excellent analyses of leadership style and process, all of which provide a wealth of information on how to assess your leadership style and adapt it to the expectations and abilities of the people you lead. And yet, I suspect that even if you have read a library of books on leadership, you still have questions. After all, very few of the books available deal specifically with leadership in human services, which presents a special challenge. It is not that existing theories about leadership lack relevance to human services, it is simply that no one has yet recognized and responded to the unique aspects of human services leadership that make your task so difficult.

If you were asked to name the human services leaders you have known and respected, you would no doubt list people who have overcome what at times seemed insurmountable odds to make things happen. The odds are unfavorable in large part because leadership authority in human services is diffuse. The U.S. Constitution assigns the power to govern to three branches of government—executive, legislative, and judicial; the human services leader is called upon to deal with all three, as well as individual constituents at the federal, state, and local levels.

Furthermore, in any human service, whether it investigates child abuse and neglect or counsels mentally ill clients, decision making is fraught with uncertainty. The nature of the client's problem is often hard to diagnose, treatment resources are limited, and human services workers must make difficult choices in a very short period of time. Often they must weigh the conflicting values and expectations of clients, human services professionals, the agency, and the community. Many families of mentally ill or retarded clients, for example, do not want these clients returned to community life, even though agency policy is based on the assumption that community living is a desired outcome. Even though teen pregnancy is a major issue in many areas, school-based health clinics that distribute birth-control assistance draw heavy fire from a variety of community groups. Some of these groups object to birth control on moral or religious grounds; some do not believe that the public school is the proper site for family planning.

The human services leader is expected to provide the direction that will enable workers, supervisors, and managers to focus their energies on solving difficult individual and community problems in an environment increasingly characterized by rising demands for services, declining resources, and strident calls for accountability. The press, government audit agencies, and a variety of community groups regularly monitor the activities of the human services agency, each holding the agency accountable according to its own interpretation of the agency's mission.

These constant demands on leaders account for the special challenges presented by leadership in human services, challenges that leadership studies have not yet fully explored. Nowhere is there a simple, coherent analysis of how human services leaders can come to grips with the full set of problems that complicate their lives. I hope this book will fill that void by providing a straightforward approach to help leaders focus the otherwise diffuse energy of a human services agency in ways that will benefit both clients and the community at large.

It is appalling to think that agencies with thousands of employees and billion-dollar budgets can be paralyzed by constraints. Yet how many times have you encountered bureaucratic inertia or read in the newspaper of agencies' failing to respond appropriately to compelling community problems? It happens all too often, because it is so difficult to sustain effective leadership authority in an agency that is constantly buffeted by class action suits, legislative inquiries, budget reductions, changing federal policies, and high levels of staff turnover. Some of our largest and oldest public and voluntary agencies have been immobilized by such forces, and their leaders are looking for ways to respond. It is often said by those inside and outside human services agencies that in this field the task of leadership is impossible. Not only is that statement demoralizing; it is untrue. The role of the human services leader can be among the most rewarding and useful in our society. This book should help human services leaders in these difficult times chart a sure course toward effective leadership.

Audience

This book is written for human services practitioners, whom I respect greatly. It is not, however, without interest to the serious student of public management. As Behn (1986) has written, since public management has only recently become a field of formal study, we must pay careful attention to the growing body of case studies and tease from them general rules for management and leadership. Behn suggests that perfecting your abilities in public management is like improving your skill at chess. You must practice, study the moves of the masters, and recognize in the situations and challenges you encounter the enduring principles that make for sound strategy.

There are as yet few books on public management. This book, based as it is on careful observation of many case studies over several years, can make a contribution to the developing knowledge in the field. Some of those case studies—drawn from human services work in Florida, Maine, Missouri, North Carolina, and Illinois—are described in the book to illustrate the effective practice of leadership, a subject of interest to practitioner and student alike.

Overview of the Contents

Leadership in Human Services details the processes of articulating and implementing a vision. In Chapter One I explain the special challenge of leadership in human services. In Chapter Two I discuss how leaders can articulate a vision and how they can adapt their mission to the grain of history. In Chapter Three I explain how forecasting can provide a way to identify the currents in human services to which programs should respond.

Chapters Four through Seven describe the steps leaders should take to translate their vision into specific objectives for delivering services to clients. These steps help to build accountability, reliability, and predictability and constitute a new way of thinking about human services—*results-oriented management*—which provides a straightforward means for cutting through the red tape of human services and actualizing your vision. The six steps of results-oriented management are

1. Identify the clients to be served and the problems to be addressed.
2. Identify the desired client outcomes for those services.
3. Decide what agency activities are necessary to produce the desired outcomes.
4. Acquire, allocate, and manage agency resources to accomplish these critical activities.
5. Monitor the critical activities closely.
6. Evaluate services regularly to make sure that critical activities are leading to desired outcomes.

Results-oriented management may not appear revolutionary, but it is a simple, powerful tool for focusing the energy of human services networks on important goals. Combined with your articulation of a vision, it is a blueprint for effective leadership. Its strength lies in its simplicity. I am convinced that results-oriented management is a useful step toward distilling principles for public management from anecdote and management lore. Results-oriented management can work—in fact, has worked—in the human services environment, where so many other approaches do not. Chapter Eight demonstrates just why this is so.

In Chapter Nine I discuss how to keep your vision alive and your programs responsive to changing demands. In Chapter Ten I talk about how leaders can create a climate that fosters change and innovation in human services. Finally, Chapter Eleven contains a few reflections on success and survival in the art of leading in the human services field.

Acknowledgments

This book has resulted in large part from the work of the National Child Welfare Leadership Center, School of Social Work, University of North Carolina, Chapel Hill. A grant to the center from the Edna McConnell Clark Foundation enabled me to write the book. The method of results-oriented management was developed during a series of executive and leadership programs offered by the center. Therefore, I must thank the principals at the center, Keith Schafer and Carol Williams, who were its first and second directors, as well as Ray Kirk and Ann Sullivan, for their guidance, support, and criticism. My debt to Keith is especially great. He was the source for many of the ideas included here, and, but for his appointment as director of the Department of Mental Health in Missouri, would have been a coauthor. I would also like to thank Peter Forsythe of the Clark Foundation for his confidence in all of us, and Emma Beckham for her cheerful and dependable technical support in producing the manuscript. I am indebted to the executives and managers who have participated in the center's programs for their inspiration and to my wife, Katrina, for managing our household and children so that I could get to know those inspiring leaders. I dedicate this entire effort to Dwayne Harrington, whose death from neglect in 1981 compels me to do what I can to enhance leadership in human services.

Rocky Mount, North Carolina   Leslie H. Garner, Jr.
December 1988

The Author

Leslie H. Garner, Jr., is president of North Carolina Wesleyan College. He received his A.B. degree (1972) in history from the University of North Carolina and his M.A. and Ph.D. degrees (1974 and 1985, respectively) in public policy from Harvard University.

Since 1984, Garner has been a senior consultant with the National Child Welfare Leadership Center at the School of Social Work, University of North Carolina, Chapel Hill. He helped found its Senior Executive Program and Children's Services Leadership Program and has served as a member of the center's core faculty.

Before assuming the presidency of North Carolina Wesleyan College, Garner was a member of the business administration faculty at the University of North Carolina, Chapel Hill, where he also served as founding director of the Government Executives Institute, an executive development program for senior managers in state and local government.

Garner has written numerous articles on the management of public services, with a special focus on human services. He has served as a consultant with state, local, and voluntary human services agencies in eleven states.

Leadership
in Human Services

1

❧❧❧

Leadership Challenges
in Human Services

The on-line catalogue at Davis Library at the University of
North Carolina in Chapel Hill lists over five hundred entries on the
subject of leadership. It might be bold to contend that none of them
deal specifically with leadership in human services, but it would
probably be realistic. In spite of the fact that much of governmental
activity in our society involves the delivery of health, education,
mental health, and other human services, there is a void in our
understanding of the special difficulties inherent in leading the
programs and agencies that provide those services.

As suggested in the Preface, the reasons that such a void
exists derive largely from the complexity of the task of leadership
in human services. Clients' problems are complex, as are the
structures of the programs that respond to them. The challenge of
focusing and directing these programs, of leading human services,
is immense but not impossible. Since this book is devoted to
helping program and agency leaders master that challenge, this first
chapter, which forms the foundation for the rest of the book,
discusses it in some detail. The working definition of leadership
developed here serves as a framework into which the ideas of the
remaining chapters are integrated. The chapter also includes a
selective guide to the literature on leadership, to show how the
theories in this book are related to that literature.

1

Let us begin the chapter with a case study of the difficulties confronting William ("Pete") Page, appointed Secretary of Health and Rehabilitative Services in Florida in early 1986. Page joined a department demoralized by a series of crises involving child abuse and neglect. His role was to rebuild confidence in the department and strengthen services to children and families. An examination of the plight he found himself in will help ground our discussion of leadership in the everyday reality of human services.

In July 1985, a three-month-old child, Corey Greer, was found dead in a foster home licensed and regularly used by the department. The subsequent investigation made public a depressing succession of errors and poor administrative decisions. Corey and his family had not received all the services they needed or to which they appeared to be entitled. They had received medical treatment because they had entered the system at a health clinic. There had been no referral to day care or family counseling and no income support. Because Corey and his sister were left alone while their parents worked, the children had been taken into state custody. Their foster mother had not known how to use the heart monitor prescribed for Corey. There were twelve children in the foster home, which had been licensed for four. Most of the workers and supervisors involved in the case had had either inadequate training or none at all.

There was evidence that the errors made in the Greer case were being repeated across the state, and the public and advocacy groups had stepped up pressure on the department to "clean up its act." The state attorney indicted the foster parents for murder. At the same time, the legislature commissioned a major study of the organization and management of the department. As the pressure mounted, more and more discussion centered on the quality of "leadership" in the department.

Page's challenge was to identify and correct the problems brought into focus by the Greer case, to improve the agency's ability to provide competent, compassionate service. To do so he would have to reduce alarmingly high levels of staff turnover. The licensing office had stopped monitoring placements the previous year because of a staff shortage and depended on caseworkers to monitor facilities and report irregularities. Three separate units in the department—one emergency intake unit and two foster care units—had made placements to the foster home. None of the units had had more than four children in the foster home in 1985; still, none had reported to the licensing office. In the Greer case, one of the supervisors had no background in foster care and had received no training. Another had four staff vacancies to fill and simply had not thought about the possibility of overcrowding at the foster home.

Over half the supervisors in the district where Corey died had had less than one year of experience. Thirty percent of the workers had had less than six months' experience, and 67 percent had had less than a year's. Low pay and poor working conditions were cited as the major reasons for the rapid rate of turnover. Pay for caseworkers was lower than pay for comparable employees in state government and for caseworkers in other states. Secretarial help had been reduced because of funding cuts, and there was little automation to help manage case records. Friction between operating units exacerbated the effects of poor casework.

Page's challenge is representative of those faced by the leader of any human services agency. The leader must be able to create an environment in which caseworkers, supervisors, and managers can effectively devote their skills to solving client problems. Creating such an environment requires clear statements of goals so that individuals and units know what they are supposed to do; some means of monitoring activities so the agency will know how well it is doing; and a willingness to wage battles over salaries and training. It requires that the agency continually nurture relationships with other agencies that can bring additional resources and skills into play.

This may not sound like a difficult set of tasks, but we know from Page's situation, and from the experiences of many other leaders in situations like his, that any appearance of simplicity is deceptive. Not only is the environment of human services administration itself complex, whether in a public or a voluntary agency, but the problems of children and families entering the system are increasingly daunting. Like Corey Greer, growing numbers of clients suffer from multiple problems that require carefully designed, multidisciplinary responses. As with the Florida Department of Health and Rehabilitative Services, few agencies have a tradition of providing such multidisciplinary treatment. Services are usually delivered through interdependent or competing agencies that could well have been designed by Rube Goldberg.

Corey Greer had serious medical problems, and his family was beset by poverty and, it seems, tension between mother and father. To provide an effective response to his situation, the department would have had to bring together services from federal, state, and local programs whose workers now struggle with a nearly overwhelming number of rules and regulations that are always in flux and often conflict with one another.

Pete Page finds his authority limited. Arguably, there are legislators who have more influence over parts of the department than he does. Some of the executives who work for him have greater access to advocacy groups and legislators. To change policy, Page needs the support of the governor and the legislature. To get more money for workers or programs, he will have to compete with advocates of better schools and highways to win appropriations. For his programs to work well, Page needs expedient disposition of cases in the courts. Many of the services Page buys for clients are provided by private agencies, some of which have their own sources of funding. In most of what he does, Page is not making unilateral decisions about policy or practice; rather, he and his agency are at the hub of a whole set of actors and agencies whose consistent support is critical for their success.

The frustrations of trying to work through such a network of agencies are well known to government executives and students of public management. Key resources are subject to outside control and a bewildering array of rules. The budget is assembled line by line. To transfer from line A to line B requires the approval of a special legislative subcommittee. Policies governing hiring and firing, designed to protect employees from abuse, further restrict the options of leadership. As Kaufman (1977) put it, one person's due process becomes another's red tape.

Certainly, much of this complexity does stem from the intergovernmental nature of the service delivery system. Lynn (1980, p. 4) offers a concise and illuminating history of the growth of human services programs and the emergence in the 1970s of what

Elliot Richardson called "ballooning overhead, prolonged delays and endless aggravation" in the growth of categorical human services programs. Derthick (1970) describes how this growth had hamstrung federal authorities in their dealings with state officials. Lynn (1980) describes the frustrations of several states as they tried to cope with complexity through reorganization. A decade and a half of attempts to reduce complexity and improve accountability in this programmatic morass have yielded percious little.

The human services professional thus faces an awesome challenge in bureaucratic and political leadership. Drawing on a rich literature in organization studies, Allison (1970), in a classic work, describes the complexity of governmental decision making in two models that show public management to be far from a simple, rational exercise. In his organization process model, public decisions result from repertoires of standard operating procedures that take on a life of their own and seem to escape the control of any single individual. In his bureaucratic politics model, decisions result from intense bargaining among actors with varied interests and bases of power. In an excellent set of studies, all focused on human services programs, Bardach (1972, 1977) and Pressman and Wildavsky (1973) show that directing the set of semiautonomous actors that make up a human services system is anything but a simple task. In fact, Pressman and Wildavsky observe that "the apparently simple and straightforward is really complex and convoluted" (p. 93). They observe that, in implementing policies, we fail to appreciate the number of steps involved, the number of participants whose interests must be taken into account, and the number of decisions that must be made, arguing that these constitute a "geometric growth of interdependencies over time" (p. 93). Lynn (1981) concludes that to succeed, the government executive must be prepared to bargain at several levels, to win the political games that determine strategy, policy, and operations.

This complexity puts a premium on leadership. Nothing of importance seems to happen in the absence of a skilled, energetic leader. At the program, agency, or superagency level, vision, determination, and political savvy are required. In policy formulation, Bardach (1972, p. 5) tells us that we need an entrepreneur with "efficiency, inventiveness and creativity" if we are to overcome the political barriers to authorizing new approaches to service delivery. Bardach (1977) observes that the leader must be able to "fix" the governmental process when political and organizational pressures push it off track in the implementation stage.

Given these observations, it is surprising that we don't know more about how to lead human services programs, about how to confront the challenge those programs present. As Doig and Hargrove (1987) observe, studies of governmental process have focused more on the process itself than on the skills of leadership required to direct it. Their collection of biographies of a dozen effective government leaders is an important contribution, as is the growing literature on leadership and entrepreneurship in the public sector. These studies suggest that though leaders in government have different backgrounds and styles, they do have certain traits in common. For Doig and Hargrove, successful government leaders are able to accomplish six tasks. They identify new missions and programs, develop and nourish external constituencies, create internal constituencies to support their programs, enhance the organization's technical expertise, motivate and provide training for staff, and systematically scan the organization to identify and protect the agency from areas of vulnerability. The best of their leaders have the rhetorical skill necessary to articulate goals and new programs and the administrative skill necessary to build strong organizations and political constituencies to support them.

Behn (1987a, 1987b), Bardach (1987), and Leman (1987) lend weight to Doig and Hargrove's assertions. Their studies all find that leaders must be good managers and must be able to articulate a viable strategy for their organizations, which they must then be able to develop by providing direction, motivation, and training for their staffs. Furthermore, they must have an astute sense of timing and political opportunity in the articulation of strategy and in day-to-day management. In a sense, these observations are not news. As Clemens and Mayer (1987, p. xiii) observe, "the problems that are central to effective leadership—motivation, inspiration, sensitivity and communication—have changed little in the past 3,000 years." What has changed, as Pete Page discovered, is the context. Human services are delivered in the complex world of intergovernmental dealings, political intrigue, and uncertainty about outcomes and interventions.

Page's organization demonstrates the complexity and bureaucratic inertia that Allison (1970), Bardach (1972, 1977), and Lynn (1981) describe. To solve the web of problems evidenced in the Corey Greer case, Page must exhibit the leadership qualities described by Doig and Hargrove (1987), Behn (1987a, 1987b), Bardach (1987), and Leman (1987). He must articulate a mission around which his department will rally. He must build an environment in which the department's workers will have the knowledge and motivation to go beyond routine to deliver effective service, where foster care units will care enough about clients not to overload a foster home, where advocacy groups and legislators will work to help provide the resources required to offer families such as Corey's the income support and counseling they need. At its simplest, then, Pete Page's task is to do what he can to create an environment inside his large organization that will foster compassion and encourage talent when a worker encounters a child and family. Yet Page does not supervise the worker or the worker's supervisors directly. He must daily go forth and do battle with advocacy groups, the budget and personnel offices, the legislature and legislative staff, and the press, often over issues that are quite remote from the caseworker trying to help Corey Greer. Some of his own executives may not listen to him, or they may try to "wait him out." They may not care, or they may be so bogged down in standard operating procedure that they are dispirited. Even those who are highly motivated—and if the Florida case is representative, there are plenty of capable, motivated managers in human services—they may not know how to manage such a broad array of programs with what appears to be so little authority.

That is where this book comes in. Page's situation, and that of the program and agency leaders who face similar problems every day, is not impossible, just difficult. In human services, energy is diffuse and programs often lack direction. This book develops a framework to help leaders focus the energy of human services and chart a manageable course through the complexity that is so clearly a part of their lives.

A Working Definition of Leadership

The first step in building a framework for effective leadership in human services is to furnish a working definition of leadership appropriate to the challenges. In *Leadership,* James McGregor Burns (1978, p. 18) writes that leadership is exercised when "persons with certain motives and purposes mobilize, in competition or conflict with others, institutional, political, psychological and other resources so as to arouse, engage and satisfy the motives of followers." Burns's essential point is that the purpose of leadership is to engage followers in the pursuit of a common purpose.

For Burns, the term *leadership* refers to two types of interaction between leaders and followers. The first, which he calls *transactional leadership,* has to do with the day-to-day exchanges of resources that essentially make things happen. A leader in human services must establish a working system of such exchanges so that the individuals, programs, and resources required to solve a problem can be matched with that problem. The leader must be able to manage budgets and organizations in order to keep programs running smoothly. Yet just to see to it that a system exists and works smoothly is not leadership. In *Presidential Power,* Neustadt (1980) distinguishes between presidents who are chief clerks and those who are leaders. Those who only keep the system functioning smoothly are merely chief clerks. They don't lead, they administer.

To lead, the president has to imbue the operating system with purpose, to exercise what Burns calls *transformational leadership,* which he defines as doing no less than establishing a quality of interaction between followers and leaders that guides both to a higher plane of morality. For Burns, transformational leadership establishes depth of purpose, linking leader and followers in activities that satisfy their need for an enduring sense of community and meaning. Neustadt argues that the choice of purpose is the first criterion for evaluating a president's performance, that the effective president must articulate a sense of purpose that runs with the grain of history and is relevant to the times.

Leaders, then, must be visionaries and managers. They must be able to articulate for their followers an inspiring vision for collective effort. They must also make things happen so that the collective purposes of leader and followers can be achieved. Simply keeping the machinery well oiled will not satisfy the need for leadership. At the same time, a grand vision, even a noble vision, is by itself insufficient. The leader who articulates a clear and relevant vision but cannot implement it is only a prophet. Consider the leader of the state mental health system who perceives the need to serve chronic patients but cannot build consensus among staff as to which diagnoses qualify as chronic or what treatment process makes sense. He or she does little more than cry in the wilderness of bureaucratic inaction. The community mental health center that provides outpatient counseling to the so-called "worried well" while chronically ill patients go untreated on the streets is hardly more effective. Even though the services may be excellent, they may not be what the community desires and thinks it is paying for.

Of course, there are those who have neither a strong sense of direction nor the skill to see the vision implemented effectively. These crisis-driven managers make decisions and shift resources in response to the latest disaster. It could be argued that Pete Page has inherited a crisis-driven organization in Florida. He finds himself in charge of an agency that has a grand but vague sense of purpose and cannot offer the services stipulated in its charter.

This book helps the leader in human services articulate a sense of purpose and build a system of daily interactions among followers that will lead to the achievement of that purpose. The leader's role is not unlike the role of an architect in the construction of a grand new building. The architect must have a vision of the way the building can fulfill an established purpose, making the best use of available space and resources. Yet no architect would trust that vision to memory or to a few notes jotted down on the back of an envelope. The architect must translate that vision into a set of operating plans that will help carpenters, electricians, plumbers, painters, and decorators ply their own specialties, often working independently, in a way that leads to the construction of a harmonious whole.

Just as the architect's operating systems are drawn up as blueprints, so the leader in human services has a responsibility to provide a blueprint for all the various people who must act in concert to help clients. The leader's blueprint is for a system of interaction among individuals and units inside and outside the agency that can bring resources together to solve client problems. And, just like the blueprint for the building, the leader's blueprint must start with a vision, a vision that incorporates enduring principles from the past but can translate them into bold approaches to new problems.

Here is where this book parts company with many other books on leadership. It does not deal with the individual's leadership style or the way the leader is viewed by his or her followers. There is already a distinguished body of literature that examines the leader's interpersonal role within the organization. It dates back at least to Argyris (1953) and includes classic works by Hersey and Blanchard (1982) and Hersey (1984), popularized by Blanchard, Zigarmi, and Zigarmi (1985). Those works describe a theory of situational leadership, which suggests that a leader's style must be a function of the followers' maturity level and of the leadership situation itself. This book does not argue with that or other theories; rather, it seeks to complement them. I propose a broader framework for evolving a vision and a management philosophy within which assessments of management style can be made.

The book also does not inquire into the intellectual foundations of leadership in government. Others, including Burns (1978) and Neustadt (1980), have already built a solid foundation there. What it does is give a simple formulation to the ways in which the supervisors, managers, executives, and advocates who lead human services can prepare themselves to articulate a vision and then translate that vision into operating systems that coordinate an exceedingly complex set of program resources to provide effective service delivery.

Is Leadership Management?

This book is addressed to managers, and yet it professes to be about leadership. I have just suggested that leaders were good managers. Are leadership and management the same thing? Do you become an effective leader simply by being a good manager? The answer is not as simple as it may seem. At least three provocative essays debate this very point. They all help us understand that leadership has some very special qualities that distinguish it from management.

In his essay "Can Managers Be Leaders?" my colleague Jack Behrman (1986) argues that leadership, management, and administration are in fact very different activities. Management, he theorizes, is the allocation of resources to achieve an agreed-upon purpose. It does not necessarily entail defining that purpose, but simply fitting together all the resources necessary to accomplish a goal. Administration, on the other hand, is the process of allocating resources in such a way as to avoid wasting them. It is the product of control systems, scheduling, and accounting. For Behrman, leadership can be differentiated from management and administration by the fact that leaders articulate a mission. They provide a vision, an overriding goal and purpose that, as Burns reminds us, inspire both leaders and followers to enhance the dignity of society and the individual.

Saleznick (1977) makes a similar observation. He sees managers as trustees of an institution, the stewards of goals, processes, and organization members in the pursuit of common goals. The manager is inherently conservative, seeking to preserve and strengthen the status quo. Leaders, on the contrary, seek to shake up what exists, try new ideas, and ask questions that direct the organization to new, often unexpected heights. They challenge and excite followers.

Finally, in their analysis of some ninety leaders, Bennis and Nanus (1985) contend that the distinction between managers and leaders is critical. Managers, the authors explain, do things right; leaders do the right things. Leaders are visionaries. They change the metabolism of their organizations, introducing new ideas, policies, and methods suited to changing times. Leaders articulate a vision that provides focus and infuse daily activity with meaning by communicating that vision to others. They build trust in their vision by building an organization that can provide accountability, predictability, and reliability. They live their vision themselves and lead by example.

None of these three essays argues that managers cannot be

leaders, but all clearly indicate that leadership is more than just good management. They all support the notions of Burns and Neustadt that leadership requires both vision and implementation. Without vision, say the Proverbs, the people perish. The leader must be able to provide a sense of purpose and then construct a management system that will focus the energies of followers on that purpose.

Human services managers must be leaders. Because human services are delivered through networks of public and private organizations, they can be led effectively only from inside. Especially in times of challenge and change, the managers of such agencies must have the vision to take risks and help move their agencies into new ways of thinking and serving that respond to the changes taking place around them.

I agree with Bennis and Nanus's (1985) assertion that leadership need not be a rare skill—that leaders can be developed; and that leaders need not be charismatic—that leadership need not be manipulative or exist only at the top of an organization. Especially in human services, leadership should pervade an organization. Commitment to clients, service, employees, and the public—not manipulation—is the crucial element of this theory. Leadership can be learned, in the sense that a systematic approach to strategy, planning, and management can be integrated into a blueprint for a program or agency. In addressing myself to leaders, I am talking to managers who should be leaders. When I make a prescription for better management, that prescription is always intended to establish and enhance leadership.

2

❧❧❧

How Effective Leaders
Articulate a Vision

In the first chapter, we proposed that a major component of leadership is the transformational task of articulating a vision, of establishing a direction of leaders and followers to pursue jointly. It makes sense to begin our prescription for leadership in human services with a discussion of how leaders should articulate a vision. Without vision, even the effective transactional leader is little more than a clerk.

In coining the term *transformational leadership,* Burns (1978) set a stiff challenge for leaders in any field. He would have leaders raise followers to a higher level of morality, inspiring in them a sense of common purpose. Transformational leadership is based on a set of principles deeply held by a society, such as those of liberty, equality, individual dignity, and justice. Burns believes that leaders should actively choose purposes that correspond to these community values: "The ultimate test of practical leadership is the realization of intended, real change that meets people's enduring needs" (p. 461).

The appearance of greatness, the ability to cloak self-interest in the rhetoric of some noble purpose, is easier to acquire than true leadership. Indeed, when Neustadt (1980) begins to assess presidential performance, he looks not at the ideology, intentions, or passions of presidents, but at the purposes to which they commit their energies and those of their followers. He writes, "Never mind the private thoughts, his preferences for one thing or another, never mind his taste for passionate display—taking the real world as he found it, what attracted his commitment in the sense that he identified himself beyond recall?" (p. 150).

Neustadt gives John Kennedy high marks for committing himself to trying to "get the nuclear genie back in the bottle," to civil rights, and to economic growth. He sees those as "precisely right as the preeminent concerns for the first half of this decade" (p. 152). Indeed, in Burns's terms, Kennedy's concerns do seem precisely right: they all derive in large part from the principles of justice, human dignity, and individual welfare that Burns believes are so important to transformational leadership.

Yet all of this is frightfully abstract. What does the idea of transformational leadership mean in a hectic world of conflicting values? How can the program manager or agency executive go about selecting and articulating a purpose that has the elevating properties Burns esteems and that is right for the times? Fortunately, these questions can be partly answered by example.

Perhaps the most prescient vision of human services in this century was Franklin Roosevelt's, and there is no better example of how to go about identifying and articulating purpose than Roosevelt's espousal of Social Security. Roosevelt raised the issue of old-age pensions while he was candidate for governor of New York in 1928. He made little progress as governor, which is not surprising. Only fifteen states had any type of old-age assistance at the time, and the average payments in those programs was only $16 a month.

By 1934, with many of his proposals to put people back to work under way, Roosevelt had created a Cabinet Committee on Economic Security, with Labor Secretary Frances Perkins as chair. He appears to have selected Perkins because he respected her knowledge of similar programs in Europe. He included on the committee the Attorney General and the Secretary of the Treasury, to deal with matters of legality and finance, respectively. After a series of meetings involving experts from around the nation and an all-night bargaining session at Secretary Perkins's house, Roosevelt got his Social Security plan. The system would use current contributions to pay benefits, so as not to tie up capital needed elsewhere in the economy. Both workers and employers would contribute to the scheme, which would provide each worker with a number and an account. Both houses of Congress passed the bill with overwhelming majorities.

There are four reasons that Roosevelt achieved such success with the Social Security idea and that his choice of purpose was so right for his time. First, the idea was clear. Roosevelt wanted to provide assistance to older Americans. He had insisted to Perkins that "you want to make it simple—very simple. So simple that everybody will understand it" (Neustadt and May, 1986, p. 99). Roosevelt admitted that the creation of account numbers and an administrative hierarchy to administer the accounts was meant to provide a way for all Americans to identify with and understand the program. Furthermore, whenever Roosevelt talked about the idea, he would discuss it in terms of individuals he knew—farm neighbors in Dutchess County, New York, for example—to help people identify with the new program.

A second characteristic of Social Security was its relevance to the times. The United States was the last of the Western nations to provide some sort of old-age assistance. But now the time was right. The Townsend movement had stirred up considerable public interest in the idea, enhancing the receptivity of Congress to the proposal. Roosevelt, of course, articulated the idea in such a way as to make the most of the opportunity, setting benefit levels so the program was a clear middle alternative to the more generous Townsend proposal, earning the support of southern Democrats, who had grave misgivings about using contributions from whites to support elderly blacks.

But even more fundamental, the Social Security idea responded to the changing nature of the U.S. workplace. The movement from farm to factory had made both the nation's work force and its elderly vulnerable by removing them from the network of the rural, farm-based extended family and putting them at the mercy of a national economy that was prone to boom and crash. It is to Roosevelt's credit that he recognized and appreciated this underlying trend in the nation's economy.

The third characteristic of the Social Security Program was that it was widely supported. It was very astute of Roosevelt to create a Cabinet committee to define his idea for him. In doing so, he involved the critical actors in his administration in the design of his pet project. The group consulted with a large number of national experts to gain their support for the program, even before the president formally presented the idea to Congress. The assigning of account numbers generated a national constituency with a tangible stake in a program that, it must be remembered, represented a major departure from the traditional role of the U.S. government in income support. Within four years of its enactment, Social Security enjoyed the support of 90 percent of the American public.

The final characteristic of Social Security that concerns us here is its consistency with the rest of the Roosevelt program. Though much of the New Deal has subsequently been dismantled or become outdated, in 1934 there was a clear trend in government toward protecting U.S. citizens from the unpredictability of the economy, whether through regulation of securities or through public works employment. Social Security fit into that pattern. The New Deal, which had begun as just a phrase in an early Roosevelt speech, was by 1935 a coherent program.

Roosevelt's introduction of Social Security was a bold stroke, but such bold strokes are not beyond the reach of most leaders in human services. Of course, most leaders are not presidents with impressive congressional majorities to back them up. Yet Roosevelt succeeded in that venture not because he was such a master politician but because he articulated a program vision that was clear, relevant to his times, widely shared by people both inside and outside his administration, and part of a coherent program. With the exception of Bennis and Nanus (1985), few students of leadership have translated examples of vision from the presidential arena into the organizational context. Articulating a vision is one of the four key strategies for effective leadership that Bennis and Nanus cite. For them, vision is a "mental image of a possible and desirable future state for the organization" (p. 89) that beckons followers to join forces in order to achieve a common goal.

The elements that make a president's vision appealing are the same ones that a human services leader must strive to incorporate into any organizational goal. Bennis and Nanus remind us that an organization is "a group of people engaged in a common enterprise" (p. 90). They write: "When the organization has a clear sense of its purpose, direction and desired future state and when this image is widely shared, individuals are able to find their own roles both in the organization and in the larger society of which they are a part. This empowers individuals and confers status upon them because they can see themselves as part of a worthwhile enterprise" (p. 90). Thus, all leaders would be well advised to articulate purpose for their organizations in the same fashion that Roosevelt did for the nation. The following sections discuss what that involves.

Clarity

Clarity of vision begins with simplicity. The leader in human services must coordinate the efforts of many individuals and groups, inside and outside the agency he or she heads. Consider the demands on Pete Page. He must develop a vision in Florida that will serve as a foundation for the work of several divisions within his department and also create the framework within which can come together the efforts of other agencies of state government; private, voluntary agencies; county governments; and individuals. Only if his vision is simple enough to be understood by all will he succeed.

Page's work is cut out for him. The current statement of vision for the Florida Department of Health and Rehabilitative Services is vague and often grandiose. With regard to health care, policy documents state that the agency's mission is to protect the health of every child in Florida. While that is a laudable goal, in the absence of clarification, it causes Page trouble. Inside the department, it does not help the regional administrator establish priorities for adapting statewide programs to regional needs. It does not help a manager or supervisor set realistic performance standards for workers. Outside the department, it raises expectations that cannot be met, by setting a tone that suggests to outside agencies, some of which have a long history of providing human services, that the department can go it alone.

But Page's goal is simple—protect the health of every child. Obviously, clarity involves more than just simplicity. A simple but unrealistic vision is unsatisfactory. The vision must be not only simple but also specific: it must state what services will be provided for what clients and for what purposes. Page's vision, for example, must explicitly state that the department intends to provide primary health care to children from low-income families in order to increase their chances for normal physical development. One of the most successful community mental health agencies I know has succeeded because its leadership has made very clear the identity of the clients it is to serve and the outcomes it expects for those clients, broken down according to diagnostic group. For chronic schizophrenics, for example, it has specified the range of medical, respite, vocational rehabilitative, and housing services it provides, in order to guarantee that all clients in that category can, first, receive treatment in the community and, second, live as normal a life as possible without posing a risk to themselves or to the community.

Relevance

By many standards, Lutheran Family Services of North Carolina (LFS) would appear to be a very successful organization. LFS grew from a single staff member in 1978 to an organization with two hundred staff members and a budget of $5 million in 1985. It grew because, better than any other agency in the state, it was able to operate high-quality group homes for "Willie M. children." Willie M. children are emotionally disturbed children prone to violent behavior. For several years in the 1970s, the parents of Willie M. attempted to find care for their son. Various public agencies, including mental health and education agencies, responded that serving such children was outside their jurisdiction. Finally, the parents filed a class action suit. The settlement required that the state of North Carolina provide a range of community-based services to such children throughout the state. Because of its reputation for quality, LFS became the major provider of such care.

LFS did not set out to become a Willie M. agency; it set out to provide high-quality services to children and youth who had no other place to turn. Willie M. just happened to LFS. However, even though it had not been explicitly formulated, the LFS vision was unquestionably responsive to an emerging need in North Carolina.

Lutheran Family Services was willing to serve a growing population of children that other agencies had not served. LFS did have the foresight to implement a no-reject–no-eject policy for Willie M. children, a policy that was clearly responsive to the needs of children who had been shuttled from placement to placement, and that put LFS in the lead for serving adolescents in North Carolina. Intelligent agency leadership is not reactive. It must begin with a vision relevant to the community.

For their vision to be relevant, leaders must understand their clients and the changes that they and their communities are undergoing. Erwin Hargrove's biography of David Lilienthal (Doig and Hargrove, 1987) is instructive, in that it shows how Lilienthal built support for the Tennessee Valley Authority by emphasizing the practical benefits electricity could bring to Tennessee farmers. If Head Start is one of the few Great Society programs that has endured several cycles of budget cutting, it is in part because it answers a need in a society where educational achievement is an avenue to success and where a generation of children was beginning to lose out in our educational system. Similarly, Meals on Wheels has been a dramatic success over the past decade, for it fulfills the needs of a growing population of homebound elderly Americans.

The Shared Vision

A vision is effective only if it is shared by those who are necessary to its implementation. In most cases, that means that the articulation of vision must be a negotiated process, in which those who will implement the vision have a voice. In the mid-1970s a group of "Young Turks" took leadership positions in the Missouri Division of Youth Services. Their avowed goal was to convert a system based on institutional care into a system based on community care. However, the real power in the division rested with the superintendents of the state's large institutions. Thanks to their longevity and their employees' voting power, these administrators commanded the attention and often the allegiance of powerful policy makers. For the Young Turks to gain control, they needed to articulate a foundation for policy that would make it possible to reduce the influence of the institutions. The Young Turks proceeded with wisdom. They created a policy development group that brought together the institutional superintendents and the community advocates within the division. The policy group set about making general policies to guide the agency's future, articulating a goal that youth should be served as close as possible to their homes and that they should be served in the least restrictive setting possible. The institutional superintendents agreed with both provisions and were party to the discussion that led to their adoption.

Subsequently, the policy development group advised that to put these two policies into motion, a central admissions unit should be created in each region, to perform a triage function by assigning youth to treatment alternatives. The proposal made sense in light of the previous policy decisions. The superintendents did not argue, because of their role in developing the policies, even though the change put an end to direct admission into their institutions. Over time, the policy led to a redirection of youth to small institutions and community alternatives. Finally, it led to closing the state's two most notorious training schools. Both changes were accomplished without serious objection from the superintendents, in large part because by that point the superintendents had openly accepted the vision. To oppose closing the schools would have been to stand against the rest of the system and its established policy direction.

Had the Young Turks tried, without the policy foundation, to close the institutions directly, or even to reduce admissions to them and redirect young clients, their efforts would most likely have failed. It was only after the policy "permeated" the system that effective control over admissions and institutions could be achieved. Only after those with influence had had the chance to consider more closely the changing needs of youth in the state could the necessary changes be made. Finally, it should be noted that by the time the institutions were closed, most of the superintendents in the division supported the decision, because by then it was their policy that was being implemented. The vision was effective because it was shared.

Another example of success through a shared vision is the story of two public health nurses, Sylvia Byrd and Meredith Martin, in Gadsden County, Florida. These two nurses were convinced that low-income adolescents in that county did not receive adequate health care. Though they were concerned about a variety of health problems among teens, the adverse impact of adolescent pregnancy particularly concerned them. They further decided that the only effective way to reach this population would be through a health center at the county high school and that the center would need to provide family planning services. Aware that providing such services might elicit objections from religious groups, nurses Byrd and Martin met individually with local ministers to explain the problem and discuss solutions. They listened carefully and, interestingly, found they needed to change their proposal very little to gain support from the ministers. What they discovered was broad concern with the tragedy of teen pregnancy. Over a period of a few months, they gained considerable support for their venture. By the time they proposed the clinic to the principal and school board, support for their idea was so widespread that it was not controversial within the county. They had built a sense of shared ownership of the problem to be solved and of a shared conclusion—that a school-based health clinic was the most appropriate response.

Coherence

A vision that is specific, relevant, and shared stands a good chance of being complicated—overly complicated, in fact. For an umbrella agency the size of Page's Department of Health and Rehabilitative Services, for example, a clear statement of all the services provided would be long and intricate and, on the face of it, would violate the criterion of simplicity. For the large, complex agency, then, vision must have yet another dimension—coherence. There must be a few clear themes that integrate program-specific visions into a single, comprehensible whole. Effective leaders seem to have a knack for identifying the unifying themes in complex topics, of creating a coherent program from specific initiatives.

For example, two former governors, Christoper ("Kit") Bond in Missouri and Joseph Brennan in Maine, achieved national reputations as children's governors. Interestingly enough, although Bond was a moderate Republican and Brennan a liberal Democrat, they used similar strategies for change. They emphasized a few themes—the importance of reducing the number of children living in poverty, and the importance of screening young children for health problems, for example. Rather than present a laundry list of program-specific proposals to voters or legislators, both governors became adept at packaging complex proposals together, presenting a few clearly understood, broad program initiatives. They added a sense of coherence to what otherwise would have been a disjointed effort. The public as well as the legislature had a clear idea of what both had in mind.

For the human services leader, multifaceted programs must be characterized by just such a statement of a few simple themes. In the case of Pete Page, for example, his children's services portfolio needs a clear policy umbrella. This could be that the department should strive to keep families together during times of grave economic, physical, or emotional stress, for example, and that it should strive to improve the health of children aged five years or less in low-income families. Some other broad policy might be articulated, but it must be coherent.

Even programs that have a small staff and budget need coherence. After all, human services programs serve clients with complex problems. The leader's vision needs to be understandable to the wide range of constituencies that must support it. Head Start and Meals on Wheels are programs whose names instantly convey coherent goals. The community mental health program mentioned earlier is not so lucky—it does not have a name that describes its vision. Leaders of such programs also need coherence—a vision expressed in understandable terms, that shows clients, workers, and community what their collective future will be. A theme that works for the community mental health center is that the center assists mentally ill and mentally retarded clients in functioning to their full capacity and reduces the risk to clients and community presented by mental disability.

How Do Leaders Make It Happen?

Leadership vision is a statement of purpose characterized by clarity, relevance, joint ownership by critical actors, and coherence across interrelated activities. Leaders face many potential pitfalls in articulating such a vision. It may be so specific that followers feel the leaders are imposing their will on them. At the same time, in their pursuit of the joint ownership described earlier, followers with discretion but without direction can get lost. In the search for relevance, an organization can discard valuable traditions and skills. The process through which a leader builds a vision and avoids these pitfalls is important.

The following chapters provide a framework that the human services leader can use to articulate a vision characterized by clarity, relevance, broad acceptance, and coherence. The next chapter discusses forecasting in human services, presenting a way the leader can identify the trends to which agency programs should respond. It offers a series of steps leaders can take to refine and focus a vision, not only to take account of trends shaping the present and future but also to draft an adequate blueprint for subsequent agency activities.

3

❧❧❧

Forecasting Trends
in Human Services

The path to a vision that is clear, relevant, widely shared, and part of a coherent policy direction may be tortuous, but leaders can tread it with assurance if they begin their journey with a clear sense of what the future has in store. Developing and articulating a vision depends on the ability to see clearly those trends that will shape the future and then to forge policy consensus around them.

There is no better way to demonstrate how to identify those trends and take them into account in articulating a vision than to present the example of George C. Marshall and his introduction of the European Recovery Program of 1948, known as the Marshall Plan. Arnold Toynbee called the Marshall Plan one of the great accomplishments of the twentieth century, and Marshall's clarity of vision in proposing massive aid to Europe was indeed impressive. Partly, we can surmise, Marshall was aware that the heavy reparations imposed by the victorious Allies after World War I had contributed to the economic malaise of postwar Europe. But Marshall also realized that with Europe in a state of economic collapse (even the victorious British had suffered enormous losses), the United States, the only Allied economy still intact, was the only one in a position to help with reconstruction.

Marshall's accomplishment is all the greater in light of the fact that the United States did not have a record of such involvement. On the contrary, after World War I, Americans had turned their backs on Europe, refusing to follow President Wilson's leadership into the League of Nations. After the Second World War, of course, the world was different. Marshall, like President Truman, was at the center of an increasingly complex struggle between the United States and the Soviet Union. It seems clear that he saw the reconstruction of democratic states in Western Europe as a majority priority in defending freedom against totalitarianism. The Marshall Plan, as he presented it in his Harvard commencement address of June 1947, was a simple appeal to Americans to help end hunger, poverty, desperation, and chaos in Europe.

The Marshall Plan satisfies all four of the criteria for vision proposed in the last chapter: it was very clear and simple; it responded to the developing geopolitical trends and the humanitarian issues of the day; Marshall and Truman adroitly built a bipartisan coalition behind it, and Truman used a high-level Cabinet group to work out the details of the plan to ensure the cooperation of key agencies such as the Treasury; and finally, it fit easily into an emerging administration policy of defending democratic states in Europe.

The idea for the Marshall Plan began with an astute reading of history, Marshall's perception of the emerging crisis in Europe and the need for strong societies in Western Europe that would resist Soviet intransigence. Marshall accurately anticipated the major influence on postwar European development—namely, the potential ideological and geopolitical battle between the United States and the Soviet Union. He had the foresight to invite the Soviets to participate in the plan, an early attempt to break Soviet hegemony over central Europe and to begin the rebuilding in partnership rather than conflict. Historians Richard Neustadt and Ernest May (1986) perceptively credit Marshall with being able to see time as a stream, to contemplate possible futures with a clear understanding of the present and past from which they would emerge. This enabled Marshall not only to forecast the dimensions of the struggle to come but also to articulate an extraordinary response. The Marshall Plan alleviated poverty and suffering in Western Europe, laid the foundation for the steady economic development of our allies, and helped build societies that could contain Soviet expansionism through their own economic strength.

A second example bolsters our understanding of Marshall's contribution and brings our discussion closer to the subject of human services. One of the remarkable aspects of American political history over the past five decades has been the stability of the Social Security system. While there are several explanations for this stability, one central reason for it was the leadership of Robert Ball, a senior administrator of the system from 1952 to 1972. As Marmor's biography of Ball (Doig and Hargrove, 1987) points out, Ball was a skilled administrator who was able to balance often competing pressures as he helped expand benefit levels and expand coverage to include health care. His understanding of the demographic reality assisted him in his efforts to keep the system fiscally sound even as benefits grew. He was sensitive to the economic needs of clients and to the rising importance to them of health coverage. He further understood the political controversy surrounding federal involvement in health care and was able to help carefully craft a set of programs that paved the way for Medicare. He not only grasped how essential administrative competence was to promoting public confidence in the system but, as Marmor reports, actually exemplified that competence in his every action.

Ball has been criticized as having wielded too much influence and as having directed a too-rapid growth in benefits and in the system itself (Derthick, 1979). This criticism seemed right to the point in the early 1980s, when the system was facing a financial crisis. Yet it was Ball who emerged from semiretirement then to help fashion the reforms that have strengthened the system not only for the crisis of the '80s but for the challenge that will set in with the retirement of "baby-boomers" in the first three decades of the next century. Ball deserves credit for the apparent resilience of the system. His leadership was characterized by sensitivity to a wide range of social factors—economic, demographic, and political—that could impinge on the system. He further understood the interaction of those factors and the course of that dynamic over time. Like Marshall, he had a far-reaching understanding of the society around him and saw not only where in the stream of time he stood but where its currents were likely to carry us.

Finding the Currents

Even though clear vision requires contemplation of the future, many human services leaders and organizations resist making forecasts. Some believe that forecasting is a science to be engaged in only by experts. Others are afraid of making erroneous assumptions, or scoff at forecasting because of the errors made by others. Otto von Bismarck was once complimented on his vision and statesmanship in creating the German state. Bismarck responded by comparing leadership to steering a boat on a treacherous river. Success, he suggested, depends on locating the undercurrents that invisibly direct the flow of the river and steering by them. He cautioned leaders not to be distracted by surface eddies but to follow the stronger currents shaping their societies. Bismarck understood the art of forecasting. From him we can learn that successful forecasting depends on identifying the underlying currents in the river, not necessarily on making a precise prediction. Both Marshall and Ball certainly had that ability, which is what all leaders must strive for.

In the 1930s, the best demographers in the nation assembled to produce a forecast of U.S. population growth through 1950. Looking at the fertility rates of the 1930s, the demographers predicted with some confidence that the U.S. population would stabilize at 150 million by 1950. With hindsight, it is not hard to spot the source of their error. They had extrapolated from the experience of the 1930s, projecting the fertility trends of the Depression onto the next two decades. Had the demographers looked further back in time, they might have noticed that the population trends of the 1930s were not typical of the century. True, fertility rates had been declining before that, but at a more gradual rate than they did after 1929. The demographers were distracted by a swirling eddy on the surface.

In the demographers' defense, it is hard to see how anyone in 1935 could have predicted the postwar baby boom. There were only a few Americans predicting a major European war, and fewer still who believed that the United States would become involved. Therefore, although in predicting that the population would stabilize by 1950, the demographers disregarded a longer-term trend, their prediction was also thrown off by impending events that they could hardly have anticipated.

In 1945, President Truman's economic advisers were possessed by the determination to prevent or retard the recession they were sure would follow World War II. After all, recession had followed the First World War, when factories converted from military to civilian production. As it turned out, the advisers had to respond instead to inflation and unprecedented economic growth. While they had looked at certain historical precedents in making assumptions about the future, they had apparently missed political and sociological factors that made 1945 very different from 1919. First, price and production controls in the 1940s were effective in restricting manufacturing for civilian purposes. Second, World War II had seen an influx of large numbers of women into factory work that had generated potential family incomes that could not be spent because of production controls. Peace unleashed extraordinary consumer demand, enhanced by the years of relative deprivation during the Depression. The economic advisers did not make the demographers' error. They referred to the past, drawing on the lessons of World War I. But they did not examine the immediate context. They looked at economic factors but failed to appreciate the political and sociological factors that made 1945 unique.

On the surface, the demographers' and economic advisers' faulty predictions seem to confirm the preconceptions that many hold about forecasting—that it is impossible, since so much has to be taken into account and you may be derailed by something unexpected. How can anyone be expected to bear in mind all the factors that might affect the future? How can anyone make a reasonable forecast when a baby boom or a war might occur?

As long as leaders believe that the purpose of forecasting is to predict exactly what the future will hold, failure is likely. Such predictions simply cannot be made with much accuracy. However, visionary statesmanship does not require such predictions. Marshall did not try to predict specific events in Europe; Bismarck was not making projections about what German society would be like in 1920; Roosevelt was not making policy on the basis of what might be required in 1955. All three leaders were responding to the contemporary problems that were affecting their societies at the time—and to the underlying currents. Because all three had a rich sense of history and a broad vision of what was going on around them, they were able to avoid the traps of forecasting and think about the future in creative ways. Each made policies to respond to trends that were historically so deeply rooted that they were sure to influence the nation for years to come.

Forecasting, then, is not the contemplation of the future for the purpose of describing it. And it is not an exact science, except in the narrowest sense. While there is a rich literature on doing forecasts using mathematical models and data, and those models are useful—for forecasting weather over the next week, economic movements over the next quarter, and the speed of penetration of new products into existing markets—they are not particularly useful in helping leaders gain the long-range perspective they need. As Levin (1981) has written, "No forecasting model using data and relationships derived from past behavior, as they all do, can ever forecast anything that was not experienced in the past" (p. 27).

Effective leadership involves thinking about the future in ways that help leaders grasp the strong currents influencing their society, their community, or their organization. Leaders want for themselves and their organizations what my colleague Otis Graham (1983, 1986) describes as a rich sense of time and context—an appreciation of how the past is unfolding and how present factors interrelate. Leaders are interested in the strong continuity between the future and the past, and in the ways that the present represents discontinuity—a break with the past that will give way to new ideas and new approaches. As Neustadt (1980) and Neustadt and May (1986) would say, they want to know where they are in the stream of time. With such a perspective, leaders can help an organization articulate a vision that is relevant to the world around.

Bennis and Nanus (1985) believe the leader's vision of future possibilities must be based on an astute reading of the past and the present. The past tells the leader what has and has not worked and why. The present can tell much about the future. Many of the clients that will be served in the year 2000—and many of the programs that will serve them—are already present. So are warning signs about future changes. Bennis and Nanus believe leaders need depth perception to see the past, and peripheral vision to scan all aspects of the present to gather the knowledge they need for articulating a vision of the future.

The case of Dwight Eisenhower, another military man, illustrates how an accurate reading of time and context (or depth perception and peripheral vision) can lead to remarkable vision. By the 1950s, Eisenhower had been at the center of world politics for over a decade, and as commander of Allied forces he had met most of the world's leaders and knew the pressing world issues. He also realized that the advent of nuclear weapons and the outcome of the Second World War had changed America's place in the world. The United States could not retreat from leadership or from its position as defender of Western democracy.

Given these facts, we might assume that Eisenhower presided over a rapid expansion in military spending. Yet quite the contrary occurred, for in addition to holding a military view of the world, Eisenhower understood that many New Deal reforms had been undertaken in response to very real societal needs. Contrary to the desires of many in his own party, he did not dismantle Social Security and in fact helped expand its coverage to ten million more U.S. citizens. He appreciated the dimensions of the postwar baby boom and from the mid-1950s on pressured Congress to support public education. Despite apparent personal misgivings, he enforced the Supreme Court's decision in *Brown* v. *Board of Education,* including sending federal troops into Little Rock, Arkansas, to expand educational and economic opportunity to Americans of all races.

Yet these are not the most striking examples of Eisenhower's ability to contemplate the future in the context of the past. As consistently as any president since, he deplored the arms race and sought opportunities to control it. Although ultimately his attempts were frustrated (in part by circumstance and in part because of his early decision to base strategic defense on nuclear weapons), he nonetheless recognized that the tradeoff between critical domestic needs and arms expenditures would be a major postwar policy issue (Ambrose, 1984). He foresaw the development of a permanent defense establishment that would become heavily dependent on large, technology-based manufacturing industries. In his farewell presidential address, Eisenhower forewarned the

American public about the influence of a military-industrial complex (a term he coined) and identified a public struggle that has endured up to the present: "This conjunction of an immense military establishment and a large arms industry is new in the American experience. . . . In the councils of government, we must guard against the acquisition of unwarranted influence, whether sought or unsought, by the military industrial complex. The potential for the disastrous rise of misplaced power exists and will persist" (Ambrose, 1984, p. 612).

Adapting this kind of thinking to human services need not be difficult. There is already a relatively broad consensus about the contextual elements that must be considered in forecasting for human services. In a book about forecasting in child welfare services, Craft, Epley, and Theison (1980) state that children and their families do not exist in a social vacuum but are part of a larger social and economic context that results from the interaction of demography, the natural environment, social organization, politics and government, technology, the economy, and culture and religion. The same could be said for the clients of all human services. The challenge is to see how these factors interrelate over time.

The forecasting matrix (Exhibit 1) is a handy way for leaders and organizations to gauge the interaction of contextual factors over time. The various factors are listed as rows in the matrix. Points in time head the columns. The matrix can be used as follows. First enter a few simple, descriptive words or phrases about the present in each row of the Present column. Then complete the Past column. Although there is no set formula for how far into the past to go, I recommend starting from a date ten years before the present. For most human services, it is helpful to go back to the mid-1960s, before the major economic crises of the 1970s (inflation, oil embargos, and the like) and before many Great Society programs had been implemented. Going back to the mid-1960s allows reflection on significant economic and social changes.

The matrix's projection into the future serves an interesting purpose. While its picture of the year 2000 is unlikely to be accurate, it should bring out any significant changes between the past and the present, potentially lasting trends. In the Future column you can

Exhibit 1. Forecasting Matrix.

	Past	*Present*	*Future*
Economy (employment, world position, major industries, and so on)			
Technology (workplace, communications, home, health care)			
Politics and government			
Family structure and lifestyle			
Population and social structure (age, income, race, class, mobility, and so forth)			
International issues			

confirm whether the trends you found in comparing present and past are in fact the deep currents that Bismarck recommended following.

To develop your skill at forecasting the future in light of the past, try filling in your own hand-made forecasting matrix. Once you have filled in all the boxes, go back to each row and ask yourself, "What is the underlying trend here?" In a clear phrase or two, try to describe the flow of events from past to present, indicating your own sense of the currents to which your agency's programs will need to respond. After you have played around with the matrix for a while, read further here to get my evaluation of trends of concern to human services, as well as a brief description of how identifying those trends might affect the vision of a few representative service agencies.

The Present

Mortimer Adler (1984) echoes Dickens in characterizing the present as the best of times and the worst of times. He sees problems that are more complex and confounding than ever, such as the problem of nuclear weapons. Yet Adler also believes that because of the wealth, education, and technology we have at our disposal, none of those problems are insoluble. In my assessment, the same holds true of human services.

Our economy is in transition. Mature manufacturing industries, such as steel and automobiles, challenged by foreign firms, are in decline, and their employment levels have been dropping steadily for several years. Employment growth is to be found in services, and increasing numbers of firms have invested in technology, believing the key to success lies there. Technology is having its most dramatic effect in the areas of information processing, communications, and health care. Desktop computers make that technology accessible to nearly everyone. It is now as easy to communicate across continents as across town.

On the home front, the federal government, dominated by issues of national security and deficit reduction, has been assuming a reduced role in domestic programs. The nuclear family is becoming increasingly less representative in the United States. With nearly 20 percent of all children living in homes headed by single women and more than half of all women now in the work force, there seems to be greater demand and tolerance for different lifestyles and family configurations. The baby boom generation has grown beyond its twenties, producing a demographic "bulge" in the middle-aged cohorts. The number of elderly is expected to grow by 34 percent between 1980 and 1990, so that the median age will continue to rise throughout the decade. Americans are increasingly more mobile and ethnically diverse. According to the 1980 census, one in ten U.S. families uses a language other than English at home—Spanish in half of those homes. A steadily declining number of Americans live in the states in which they were born.

On the international scene, the United States and the Soviet Union continue to negotiate on arms control and on their economic and political future. There is great concern over debt in developing countries, and there are a number of trouble spots—the Middle East, the Republic of South Africa, the Philippines, and Central America, for example—in which the United States has clear stakes. The People's Republic of China is emerging as a major actor on the world stage.

The Past

Compare the present scenario with the world of the mid-1960s. The domestic economy was then booming, with foreign competition negligible. The effects of the Vietnam war had yet to be felt. With computer technology just coming into its own, large organizations were using giant computers. Communications satellites were only on the drawing board. Under Lyndon Johnson, the federal government was assuming a major role in human services and racial justice. The Voting Rights Act was passed in 1965, about the time that Great Society programs such as Medicare and Head Start were begun. The divorce rate was beginning to rise, and the majority of women worked inside, rather than outside, the home. There were small numbers of professional women and smaller numbers of minorities in professional jobs. Baby-boomers were in their teens. The flood of students attending college were beginning to express dissent over the Vietnam war. Migration from the rural South into northern cities continued, though at a slower rate than in the preceding two decades. The stage was set for a period of détente with the Soviet Union. Meanwhile, in the area of foreign policy, the nations' attention was focused on southeast Asia.

The Future

So much has happened since the mid-1960s, and now there is only a little more than a decade before we enter the next century. In thinking about what that century will bring, it is important to recognize the *range* of possible futures. For example, it is entirely feasible that the year 2000 could see either sustained economic growth or a significant recession. The U.S. economy is clearly in transition in an increasingly competitive world. For perhaps the first time in American history, U.S. business must adjust to global competition. Uneven growth and increased levels of business failure are likely as readjustment occurs. With use of technology spreading in all areas, will increasing numbers of Americans be denied full participation because of poverty or lack of education? And without their participation, can steady economic growth be sustained?

I believe that contrary to the opinions of some, the U.S. government will not abandon its commitment to human services. However, the commitment must change. In the short term, there is little prospect for innovative federal leadership. State and local governments must become the testing grounds for new approaches to problem solving. The global aspirations of the 1960s will surely give way to more measured attempts at solving specific problems. For instance, the California and Massachusetts programs for job training and work assistance as part of welfare can be models for greater accountability in public assistance programs and for ensuring that assistance programs are consistent with the dominant cultural values of work and individual responsibility.

Since the proportion of single-parent households is unlikely to decline, new ways will probably develop to support single parents, especially single mothers, as they juggle family and job responsibilities. The current move in Congress toward mandatory pregnancy leave seems to signal such changes. With the growing proportions of black, Hispanic, and Asian Americans, agencies must amend their standards of service and delivery.

International issues are the hardest to forecast, because, ironically, they are in many ways the most under our control. The dominant issues seem sure to be those of arms control and the relations between industrialized and industrializing nations. It is unclear whether these issues will be contemplated with the vision of a George Marshall or Dwight Eisenhower.

Trends

As guidelines for human services program development, I see the following trends.

Economics. There is a clear move toward a world economy in which science and technology play major roles and in which services are important sources of employment. Drucker (1980) terms this transition a "sea change," believing it the most fundamental alteration in the way we work since the movement from farm to factory at the end of the nineteenth century. Bell (1976) sees the economy moving into a post-industrial stage, in which information and knowledge will play an important part in work, home, and community affairs. This underscores the need for education programs as part of the human services package—for everyone from young children to adults. However, as more people take service jobs, many of them low-wage and dead-end jobs, the opportunities for true economic advancement may become limited. I believe that workers will need assistance and support in order to start their own service businesses—whether it be house-cleaning or software-writing—and thereby enjoy the economic mobility so valued by Americans.

Technology. The trend toward increased innovation in artificial intelligence, communications, memory, and health care seems clear. This raises the issues of finding new ways for the elderly to contribute to the economy, of using technology to cut through bureaucratic red tape and ensure that public and private organizations respond promptly to human needs.

Politics. I see a growing need for state and local governments to innovate and test new approaches to the problems of poverty, illness, and alienation. These tests could serve as the basis for a new round of federal initiatives. There seems little doubt that, at least through the mid-1990s, a major federal task will be controlling the budget deficit. The situation is not unlike that of the 1920s, in that states must now sponsor new programs, much as New York, California, and Wisconsin once started programs that served as the basis for the New Deal.

Demographics. The aging of the baby boom generation raises the specter of an unprecedented elderly population in the early decades of the next century. It is imperative that we help middle-aged Americans change careers and upgrade skills to stay productive. We will also need programs to help single women who head families and to provide support for children in those families, given the increasing numbers of such individuals and the strong likelihood of poverty among them. In response to increasing cultural diversity, we must preserve the integrity of our various cultural groups while still maintaining a sense of community.

International Arena. The key issues are clear—arms control and the distribution of economic and social opportunity. Within the last year, scientists have alerted us to the growing danger of environmental pollution. We may have made irreversible changes in the world's climate. The nations that have sophisticated industrial economies must consider how to manage their continued growth in a world of finite resources. All nations must consider the distribution of wealth and economic opportunity around the globe and the balance between population and economic growth. How to provide increasing economic opportunity to industrializing nations, how to expand political and social freedoms, and how to manage regional conflict in a nuclear age are pressing issues for all nations.

Managing Forecasting

What do these trends mean for human services? First, human services must place a premium on programs that will break the cycle of poverty, poor health, and illiteracy and provide a route out of the underclass culture that is building in many urban centers. Second, there is a need for more day-care and early childhood education programs. We will need increasingly innovative approaches to the problems of adolescents, who are so often the victims of family breakup. Human services will have to pay more than lip service to community alternatives for them—and for other clients as well. Agencies will need more sophisticated approaches to serving the elderly. All programs will have to be well managed and open to new delivery alternatives.

In order to gain a more in-depth look at the new directions human services will need to take, let us examine three agencies: a child welfare agency, a health care agency, and a mental health clinic. All three are community programs (as opposed to state agencies). In each case, I will briefly describe the program direction implications of trends in politics, economics, and demographics.

Child Welfare Agency. Changing demographics suggest there is a potential for conflict between elderly constituents and children in need of service. Both groups will grow in numbers, suggesting competition between them for scarce government funding. To build elderly constituencies for their programs, leaders need to recognize that investing in children secures our collective economic future. And because grandparents seem to be exercising increasing influence on child rearing and family affairs, leaders must begin to treat grandparents as part of the natural family unit and seek ways to involve grandparents in early intervention strategies. To effectively handle the changing ethnic composition of the population, agencies must make sure that their staff members are drawn from a broad range of cultural backgrounds. When a group of California child welfare leaders recently met to do some forecasting, one of them reminded the group that by the year 2000, California will be a "minority" state. Yet there was not a single black or Hispanic manager present. That must change. Changing urban demographics indicate a need for special efforts to enroll city children in early screening, day-care, and other early education programs, which are critical if those children are not to be condemned to the underclass.

The child welfare agency must recognize that children are frequently the victims of the current economic transition. Single-parent families have become common, and single parents need help—after-school programs, respite programs for single mothers, and day care. Yet given tight agency budgets and limited federal funds, these innovations will be hard to come by. Recognizing the trend toward greater state and local responsibility, the leader must be creative in using child support payments and entitlement programs as fresh funding sources for children's services. Some states, such as Maryland, have successfully expanded service availability by shifting their focus to family preservation and routing money that had gone into institutional care into home-based services. That sort of reallocation is appropriate to the trends in demographics, economics, and politics.

Health Care Agency. Political pressures to limit available resources raise problems regarding the cost of health care services, particularly Medicare. The search for care options less expensive than nursing homes, that is, for home care for the elderly, should be a priority. As demographics suggest, care for the elderly is becoming increasingly necessary, and home-based services seem the only option, given limited resources. Demographics also indicate a strong need for education programs about sexually transmitted diseases and drug use. And because the families of the working poor usually have no health insurance, orienting state and local programs to serve them is a must. Though community programs lack control over state requirements on serving the working poor, they can influence the hours and location of clinic services and thereby expand coverage. Aggressive pursuit of entitlement funding to serve the children of single women is also a necessity. In Florida, for example, where officials in one county discovered there was not a single pediatrician providing care to Medicaid patients (because the state had set the cap on payments to physicians below the prevailing rate), the local health department became the Medicaid billing agent, and physicians were then rotated throughout the clinic, providing service on contract and thereby expanding health coverage to low-income children.

Mental Health Clinic. The current limits on resources mean there is increasing pressure for accountability, especially in treating the chronically ill. Community mental health money intended for chronically ill patients should be spent on them, and community mental health leaders should pay increased attention to deinstitutionalized patients. With the economy in transition, a review of job preparation and training programs is in order. For instance, a vocational rehabilitation program in North Carolina found itself shifting from low-wage subcontracts for local manufacturers to specialized services to high-tech companies, with the result that the staff had to learn about high technology, a marketing agent had to be hired, and the agency had to shift its focus from batch work to long-term contracts. Finally, mental health leaders will find their services in increasing demand by the elderly and their families. Day programs and respite care are clear options for the future. In addition, as baby-boomers age, the number of middle-aged schizo-phrenics is rising; resources should be reallocated accordingly.

You may not agree with these assessments. You don't have to. No individual can foresee future trends perfectly. Marshall and Roosevelt made mistakes. People still remember Social Security, but how many recall Roosevelt's attempt to pack the Supreme Court? Winston Churchill, who read so clearly the Nazi threat in the 1930s and the Soviet threat of the 1940s, was much less prescient in his understanding of the evolution of the needs of the British working-class. In none of these cases did the difficulty of forecasting cause the leader to hesitate. Never was it an excuse not to probe for insights into the future or shape programs and policies that would respond to them.

On occasion, each of those leaders involved others in the forecasting process. That helps. The more people involved, the more facts and perspectives can be brought to bear on the problem. Truman and Marshall involved many people in sorting out the Marshall Plan. Roosevelt did the same with Social Security. Use of the forecasting matrix presented earlier gives you the chance to involve staff and key constituents in some collective thought about the future. I have used the matrix at large gatherings, assigning to small groups the task of completing the different rows and then having the groups compare notes. You may want to try that or some other approach. The point is that to articulate a vision, you must anticipate the future, always understanding it in reference to the past. Once that is done, you are ready to help your colleagues focus their energies on the roles they can play as the future unfolds.

4

愛愛愛

Identifying Client Needs
and Ways to Meet Them

On December 3, 1981, Dwayne Harrington, a six-year-old boy in St. Louis, Missouri, died of a major infection. His child protective services case had been closed three weeks earlier in light of what the worker described as "excellent progress." Although an abuse report had been filed on Dwayne a week before he died, no worker had seen Dwayne. The St. Louis medical examiner was rightly outraged that the child died of infection, which, if detected early, could have been treated routinely. Had the call from his school nurse been placed earlier or had the worker seen Dwayne immediately, the death could have been avoided and Dwayne, quite likely, could have been placed in a treatment program that would have given him a chance at a normal childhood.

None of this happened. The human services system failed. In fact, its behavior was chaotic and unruly. None of the collective expertise of the St. Louis human services bureaucracy was effectively brought to bear on Dwayne's case.

Tragic though it is, Dwayne's case would not deserve our consideration if it were a rare instance of system failure. Unfortunately, it is not rare. The state human services official for the St. Louis area estimated at the time that as many as 10,000 children might be in situations similar to Dwayne's in that city alone. The accumulated weight of the lack of agency focus on a vision, the lack of coordination among related services, and categorical funding and rule making had so hamstrung the agency that it could not serve its clients effectively. The considerable expertise in the system was so diffuse that it was not reaching a sizable segment of its client population.

How can the human services leader focus such energy? Surely in the Harrington case there was a clear vision of what had to be done. Dwayne needed health care; his family needed support, such as housing and training in parenting skills. Service vision was not the problem. The problem was ineffective translation of vision into action. The essential purpose of the system got lost in program and bureaucratic complexity.

The human services leader must be able to draw up a blueprint for action that can overcome such obstacles. He or she must help translate a service vision into administrative systems that focus the expertise and energy of a human services network on the needs of clients. *Results-oriented management* is a simple format for management planning that develops clarity of vision that is easily translated into workable administrative systems and client-centered focus for the human services organizational network.

Results-oriented management involves the following six steps:

1. Identify the clients to be served and the problems to be addressed.
2. Specify the desired client outcomes for those services.
3. Select critical agency activities needed for each outcome to occur, called *critical success variables.*
4. Acquire, allocate, and manage agency resources so as to perform well on the critical success variables.
5. Monitor critical success variables closely.
6. Evaluate client outcomes to ensure that the critical success variables are leading to the desired outcomes.

The logic behind the six steps is straightforward. In the first place, human services is a *client-oriented* endeavor. It exists to help clients overcome handicaps and barriers to productive and satisfactory lives. Tregoe and Zimmerman (1980) emphasize that to be successful, every organization must recognize and focus on a driving force, some aspect of its product, market, technology, capabilities, or results that will define its present and future. They consider human services a market-driven (client-driven) enterprise. Thus, clients are the driving force of human services.

As human services professionals, we have enormous resources at our disposal, yet the diffusion of authority that plagues our agencies often keeps those resources from flowing to our clients. This was the tragedy of Dwayne Harrington. We must put our clients at the forefront of our thinking so we can determine how best to direct agency services and resources to them.

Once we know who our clients are, we must consider what differences we intend to make in their lives. Our agencies fail if they exist only to satisfy measures of bureaucratic efficiency—number of people seen, number of forms processed. We believe we can make a difference, and we must lead accordingly. Therefore, we look to outcomes—changes in client welfare—as the true measure of success. As Carter (1983), Hatry, Winnie, and Fisk (1981), and Schainblatt (1977) point out, without good indicators of outcomes, we cannot allocate resources effectively or manage wisely. However, recognizing that outcomes are sometimes hard to measure and difficult to identify, we will look to those critical agency activities that, performed well, ensure that we are doing our utmost for our clients. Once identified, these critical success variables provide the basis for our planning and control systems. We are following the ideas set out by Daniel (1961), Anthony, Dearden, and Vancil (1972), and Rockart (1979) when they say that for corporate decisions to be timely and effective, executives must be able to identify the critical factors that ensure success.

Armed with a set of critical success variables, the leader can exploit the flexibility available in planning, budgeting, and information systems and thereby provide effective client-oriented discipline. That is the subject and the promise of the last three steps of results-oriented management. All six steps are described in this and the next five chapters. This chapter describes steps 1 through 3. Steps 4, 5, and 6 are dealt with in Chapters Five through Eight.

Step 1: Identifying Clients and Problems

Let's begin with the task of evaluating the work of a community physician. Suppose you are provided with a count of the number of patients seen, the number of pills prescribed, and the number of injections administered in a given year. Can you make an evaluation?

If you answered yes, you know something I don't know. How can we evaluate the impact of this service when all we know is how many medicines were given but not how appropriate they were? And we do not know what happened to the patients; we only know what the physician did.

Okay. Suppose you now discover that 90 percent of the physician's treated patients recovered. Satisfied? What if only 45 percent had recovered? Is that only half as effective as 90 percent? If this physician is a pediatrician treating mainly colds and viruses, then even a 90 percent recovery rate might not be satisfactory. On the other hand, if the physician is treating cancer, 90 percent is miraculous, and even 45 percent is excellent.

Clearly, we cannot evaluate the physician without knowing something about the patients served. Only when we know the diagnoses and what can be expected from the treatment can we begin to evaluate the physician's effectiveness.

How does all this apply to human services? Think of almost any human services organization you know. How often does the agency defend its programs in terms of, say, the number of clients it sees, the number of visits and foster care placements it makes, or the number of adoptions finalized? These are the measures equivalent to pills, shots, and patients seen. And although we decided not to judge the physician on that basis, we plan and evaluate human services in those terms all the time.

It is no wonder, then, that caseworkers are confused. And it is not surprising that the school nurse and investigative worker in Dwayne Harrington's case failed to do what was needed to help the child. Their system lacked focus. Leadership planning in human services, like planning for the physician, must begin with an explicit understanding of the clients to be served and the problems to be solved.

This is not so easy to do. For one thing, our clients are the service recipients, not legislators, taxpayers, or the like. As distinguished from clients, these latter support the service but do not receive it. They are *constituents*; and their interests are important, for those interests may determine exactly which client problems the agency tackles. But the analysis must begin with the client.

For example, suppose you are planning a clinic to provide health care to adolescents. The adolescents are your clients; the taxpayers are your constituents. The clients' problems might include poor nutrition, substance abuse, and disturbing levels of pregnancy and sexually transmitted diseases. Even though your planning must begin with a focus on these problems, your constituents may be unwilling to support public programs providing birth control, and therefore may restrict the focus of the program. Their reservations are not your starting point.

It is very important to be *explicit* about clients and problems. For instance, just who and what should be the focus of the adolescent health clinic? Adolescents have many different health-related problems. A school-based clinic could serve low-income youth who have no other access to health care. Or it could serve youth with drug- and alcohol-abuse problems. Or it could focus on teen sexuality, sexually transmitted diseases, teen pregnancy, and birth control. If the kind of clients to be served and problems to be solved are not made explicit at the outset, the clinic intended to serve low-income youth might begin serving middle-class youth. Or rather than providing general health care, it could see its resources used for dermatology cases that could be treated elsewhere.

Or consider the plight of community mental health centers. Designed to provide transition to community living for chronically ill patients, many such centers currently serve what is termed "the worried well" and face a backlash of public opinion. The clinic might also find itself providing birth-control and teen-pregnancy services when its constituents have strong reservations about both. Just as likely, it could end up trying to be all things to all clients, and serve none of them well. Without an explicit statement of its targeted clients and problems, the center will have no focus, no basis for allocating resources, and no way to demonstrate its effectiveness to those who provide its financial support.

Step 2: Specifying Outcomes

Once clients and their problems are identified, desired outcomes must be specified. Outcomes are statements of the way that clients' lives should be different as a result of the services delivered. For example, outcomes for children served by a physician include being free from those early childhood diseases for which immunizations are available, suffering only a minimum number of days of illness, and developing physically and emotionally at an acceptable pace.

To define comparable outcomes for human services, the leader and followers must answer the following question: What should clients be able to do, or how should their conditions change, as a result of our intervention? Outcomes should always be stated in terms of changes in the welfare of the client. For example, to state that children reported as being abused or neglected should be seen within twenty-four hours of the report is not a true outcome statement. This may be an admirable goal, but it is a goal for the investigative process and only implies a client outcome. The relevant outcome in this instance is that the child will remain safe during the investigation. Seeing the child within twenty-four hours is one way to make certain that the child's safety is realized as an outcome.

Outcomes should be stated in nontechnical terms that are readily understood inside and outside the agency. Their importance should be easily justified or obvious to laypersons. They should pass what I call the "grandmother rule": your grandmother should be able to understand the outcome without asking why. For example, grandmother would readily understand why you wished to keep a child safe during an investigation, but might wonder why it is so important for an agency to require workers to interview and examine a child within twenty-four hours.

The statement of outcomes is the base on which service expectations inside and outside the agency are built. Your desired outcomes will require the understanding and endorsement of elected officials, community groups, and the public. Therefore, their statement should be clear and relate directly to the identification of clients and problems.

Take as an example an adolescent pregnancy program cosponsored by a Department of Social Services, the public schools, and a coalition of voluntary agencies. Assume the program was initiated in an atmosphere of goodwill and shared intention of helping adolescent mothers but that desired outcomes were never made explicit. Pity the program director. He or she will be bombarded by queries from three major constituent groups, each of which is likely to assume an outcome based on its own parochial concern. The leader will have considerable difficulty making decisions and establishing priorities. And beware the auditor's program review when the auditor's evaluation is based on expenditures, not impact. Every one of these events could occur. None of them is inevitable, however. They are brought on by a lack of clarity over outcomes. How much better off such a program would have been if the outcomes had been explicit at the beginning.

Step 3: Selecting Critical Success Variables

Can you go straight to planning once outcomes are identified? I am afraid not. For instance, assume you had begun planning for the physician and your objective was to make sure that children developed normally. What would you do? And how would you know if what you were doing was right? What if you did nothing, and then only when the child reached adolescence did you find out that a mistaken diagnosis had been made shortly after birth? Should you therefore try to do everything for every patient to make sure that nothing went wrong? Should you try to monitor every aspect of every patient's development to ensure an effective early-warning system? No, for if you try to be all things to all patients and to monitor each child thoroughly and frequently, your program will quickly get bogged down in the details of monitoring. Yet if you monitor nothing—if you wait ten years for the outcome to occur— you will miss the opportunity for midcourse guidance.

Clearly there must be a middle course between doing everything and doing nothing. There must be some way to plan human services when the outcomes are difficult to articulate and measure, some way to organize around intermediate steps that facilitate planning, monitoring, and evaluation.

Finding such a middle course requires that leaders focus their agency on the critical success variables mentioned earlier, those few activities that, done well, ensure to the best of the leader's knowledge that the agency is on the right path toward its desired outcomes. These are similar to the critical success factors identified by Rockart (1979) in his attempt to focus the management information needs of corporate executives. Rockart's idea was that there are a few key factors that, managed closely, will ensure success on a broad range of profit and market goals. Similarly, we are concerned with variables that produce desired results, but our goals are different from those of Rockart, and they are harder to measure. Hence, our critical success variables are more than key factors in the human services process. They are key agency activities that can be monitored, even when the outcomes cannot.

Performing the critical success variables well does not mean that the desired outcomes will necessarily ensue—after all, some factors are outside the agency's control. But it does mean that the agency has done all it can to see that the outcomes are achieved. Seeing within twenty-four hours a child that has been reported abused or neglected is a potential critical success variable. The agency is interested in keeping the child safe during and after the investigation. Only if the agency sees the child promptly and is assured of a high-quality investigation is there a chance of achieving this outcome. Of course, something outside the agency's control could still put the child in danger. Nonetheless, if the agency works at seeing children promptly and making a thorough investigation and deliberate decision, it will probably have done all it can to ensure the child's safety. Therefore, it is reasonable to use promptness and quality as critical success variables.

From the many things an agency could do to influence a desired outcome, the leader must select only the most important for the agency to focus on. Critical success variables must therefore have the following characteristics.

1. The total number of critical success variables for any outcome must be small. The more variables an executive or agency tries to implement and monitor simultaneously, the more likely it is to get bogged down or spread its resources too thin. The critical success variables are a means to an end, not an end in themselves.

2. Critical success variables should be easily understood. They should pass the "why" test. When a layperson asks why a

critical success variable is important, the leader should be able
to make the connection to the desired outcomes in a single
sentence. For instance: "We see children within twenty-four
hours because it is the best way to keep them safe while we
investigate the report."

3. Critical success variables can be monitored. It would be nice to
    manage by outcomes—to keep client interests clearly up front
    in the agency. But outcomes sometimes cannot be measured.
    They are often subject to factors outside the agency's effort.
    Think how confusing it is to caseworkers and others when they
    have no reliable way to tell whether they are doing the right
    thing, or whether they are doing the right thing even though
    available evidence suggests that they are not. By monitoring
    agency activities that are clearly related to desired outcomes,
    you can avoid such problems.

4. Criticial success variables must be believable to contribute
    directly to the achievement of desired outcomes. They must
    represent the very latest understanding of how human services
    intervention can improve client welfare. There will be some
    uncertainty in the relationship between variables and out-
    comes. After all, there is much that is unknown about many of
    the problems we deal with in human services. The specification
    of critical success variables can and should change as new
    knowledge is discovered. But at any point, critical success
    variables should represent the agency's best bet as to what it can
    do to serve its clients.

5. Critical success variables should act as a "driving force" for
    other agency activities. Ensuring high performance on a
    critical success variable should ensure high performance in
    other, related activities. For example, if a clinic is to see a child
    within twenty-four hours of reported abuse, reports must be
    complete and accurate, and be processed promptly. By empha-
    sizing prompt attention to the child, the leader is also attending
    to other aspects of the investigation.

A Note on Change

Critical success variables are not static. There are at least
three situations in which they can and should change. First, clients

change. For example, Willie M. children are maturing out of the original age bracket. This change presents two problems. It brings to the agency a new client need—in this instance, transition to adult life. Such new needs demand the specification of new outcomes and identification of new success variables. In this case, a new desired outcome is effective transition to adult community life. One possible critical success variable is the completion of a transition living experience.

Critical success factors also change when outcomes change. In the case of Willie M., suppose it were found that the inappropriate behaviors were caused by chemical imbalance and a new drug were developed that could eliminate the imbalance. Rehabilitation might become the desired outcome, as opposed to stabilization of behavior. For several decades, the desired outcome in foster care was protection of the child. The critical success factor was separation from the dangerous home environment. As permanency-planning policies developed (see below), policy makers were, in fact, expanding their set of desired outcomes to include protecting the integrity of the family. A different set of success variables was clearly in order.

Foster care also illustrates the third reason critical success variables change. They change when evidence accumulates that the critical success variables do not lead to desired outcomes. In the case of foster care, separation from the family did not necessarily lead to protection of the child. In fact, there was increasing evidence of harm to the child in extended or multiple foster placements. Therefore, a new program focus was needed—on family preservation (keeping families together) and permanency planning (as quickly as possible reuniting families that had to be separated due to the seriousness of abuse and neglect, or, if return home is not possible, termination of parental rights and adoptive placement of the child).

An Example—Services for Adolescent Mothers

The derivation and use of outcomes and critical success factors can be illustrated by the relatively simple example of designing a program to serve first-time adolescent mothers. Assume the following:

You are the chief executive of a large, multiservice voluntary agency in an urban county. You have cultivated a positive working relationship with the county Department of Social Services (DSS), which contracts with you regularly for a variety of services. DSS has received an allocation through the county Children's Trust Fund to support community prevention efforts. The citizens' board administering the fund has requested that the county develop a program to help at-risk teenagers who are first-time mothers. In the past five years the number of births to county teenage girls has increased by over 60 percent. The increase has been particularly steep among those between fourteen and sixteen years old. While the rate has remained high for black and Hispanic teens during the five-year period, percentage growth has been greatest among white teenagers. The number of teenage mothers without parental or other means of support has also increased dramatically during this time. Pregnancy is the largest single reason that girls drop out of junior and senior high school in the county. While the public school does not have a special policy suspending pregnant girls or mothers from attending, it makes no special provision for them.

DSS has no experience in designing or administering programs targeted at adolescent mothers and their children and has asked your agency to submit a proposal for a contract to serve up to twenty-four teenage clients who are about to have a child or who have a child under three months old. While DSS does not have specific recommendations regarding program goals, action plans, evaluation criteria, or costs, they have provided the following demographic and related information.

County statistics show that for the target population, there is a 25 percent chance that the babies will be born prematurely; a 50 percent chance that a second pregnancy will occur within two years of the first birth; an 80 percent chance that the mother will not complete high school; a 70 percent chance that she will remain on public income assistance four or more years after the birth of the first child; and a 35 percent chance that within five years after the birth of the first child she will be referred for alleged child abuse or neglect, predominantly medical neglect or inappropriate parenting skills.

Statistics also show that most of the fathers are known, even though few of the couples are married. Ninety percent of the fathers are under twenty-one years of age. Past experience suggests that 20 percent of the mothers will marry the father of their first child within three years of the child's birth, but that only 25 percent of the fathers will make any contribution (money, gifts, food, clothing, or the like) to the mother or child within the first two years of the child's life.

Now test yourself. Try your hand at steps 1 through 3 of the results-oriented management format. On a sheet of paper, mark four columns. Head the left-hand column "Clients," the second column "Problems," the third column "Outcomes," and the right-hand column "Critical Success Variables." Fill in the chart, starting with clients. Identify client groups and note their problems. Specify desired outcomes for each client group. From the outcomes, try to derive what you believe are critical success variables.

Fill in the chart before you read the following. The chart may not be exactly right, but it should help you master the first steps of the model.

Step 1: Identifying Clients and Problems. There are at least four client groups for this program. First, there are the teenage mothers themselves. Their needs are several. They should have a successful delivery. Their physical, educational, or employment development should not be impeded by the child. They should not become estranged from family and community. They should be able to develop their parenting skills.

A second client group is the children. They need a successful delivery and effective perinatal development. They need bonding with parents to begin their own physical and emotional development.

A third group is the fathers. There are legitimate issues with regard to their rights and responsibilities, their awareness of these responsibilities, and arrangements to meet them.

Finally, there are the grandparents, whose roles with respect to parents and grandchildren are at issue.

Step 2: Specifying Outcomes. For each of these client groups, there are a few clear outcomes desired, which relate directly to the clients and their needs. For the mothers, desirable outcomes are personal development, adequate parenting (including providing the child with economic, medical, emotional, and educational support), and no repeat pregnancies within two years. The desired outcomes for the child are bonding with the mother and normal development. The desired outcomes for the father are understanding of his rights and appropriate support for mother and child. For the grandparents, the desired outcome is support for the parents and the child.

This is neither the only nor the perfect set of desirable outcomes. Different programs serve different clients and lead to different outcomes. For instance, a program sponsored by a health department could legitimately focus on health outcomes; one in a public school might emphasize education. In any case, though, the outcomes must be explicit.

Step 3: Selecting Critical Success Variables. There are two or three agency activities that are critical to achieving each of the outcomes identified. For example, for the outcome of adequate parenting, a critical success variable might be successful completion of a parenting course. That is an easily defined and monitored agency activity that, if completed, should benefit the client. The critical variables corresponding to the outcome that mother and child remain healthy might be effective enrollment in health care services, combined with training in how to use the services.

These are critical success variables over which the agency has control and which, if met, would in your best judgment lead to the outcomes you desire. Once you select them, you are ready to direct agency resources toward the outcomes. Using critical success variables to focus management strategy is the subject of the next chapter.

Now that you have completed this test case, you are on your way to mastering results-oriented management, which can help you focus power and authority and thereby accomplish your leadership mission. Such focus is made possible by the choice of a few key activities around which agency energy can coalesce.

Setting Critical Success Variables in Your Agency

If you are tempted now to take a sheet of paper and begin identifying clients, outcomes, and critical success variables for your agency, please resist. How would you feel if your boss came in and told you that from now on you were to manage according to his or her ideas about what you are doing? Even if your boss is an acknowledged expert in the field, you would probably resent not having the chance to use your own program experience to develop a planning and control framework for "your" program.

All along, we have thought about leadership as setting up a blueprint for coordinating the activities of others. Your best guarantee that the blueprint will be followed is the ownership of the blueprint by the professionals you must trust to implement it. They can gain ownership if they are allowed to think through clients, outcomes, and critical success variables for themselves. Let them think through the difficult choices their programs present in the identification of clients and problems. In reviewing their work, share with them your own views of the appropriate clients for their services. Then repeat the process for outcomes and again for critical success variables. You may be surprised at the disagreements and policy issues that arise. At the end, you will have a much clearer vision of what each program, and the agency itself, is supposed to accomplish. You will be ready to use critical success variables to strengthen your planning, budgeting, and monitoring activities.

5

❦❦❦

Establishing Priorities
and Performance Standards

In the last chapter, I made the case that the leader can successfully direct the human services enterprise by setting and monitoring performance expectations that have been articulated for client outcomes. The idea is that managing for results is only possible if desired client outcomes are articulated in advance. The leader then needs to direct a planning and monitoring process that helps everyone in the agency understand how his or her efforts are producing those desired outcomes.

The last chapter ended with a walk through the first three steps of results-oriented management: identifying clients, selecting desired outcomes, and enumerating critical success variables.

Now we turn our attention to how to use critical success variables to enhance leadership authority. The last three steps of the results-oriented management model do just that. Planning, resource allocation, monitoring, and evaluation become powerful leadership tools when you have mastered critical success variables. They provide the mechanisms for focusing attention and making things happen.

There is no mystery as to why the latent power of critical success variables is loosed in the context of planning, budgeting, monitoring, and evaluating. When you consider what authority human services leaders have, you rather quickly discover that leaders are given wide latitude over the design and implementation of information systems, planning processes, program evaluation efforts, and—albeit within formal constraints—the management of budgets. Without critical success variables, these various activities often proceed independently. They need to be coordinated, in the way that the various sections of an orchestra are led by the conductor. Outcomes and critical success variables put the human services leader in the position of conductor, baton in hand, ready to lead. This chapter and the following three demonstrate how results-oriented management can enhance your leadership authority. This chapter deals with the way that outcomes and critical success variables can focus your planning effort. The next three show how outcomes and critical success variables can do the same for your budgeting, monitoring, and evaluation activities.

What Planning Is and What It Is Not

Most of us plan, but few of us behave as if we have a plan. Nearly everyone understands what good planning is all about. The problem, unfortunately, is that not many agencies implement the planning steps well. We fill out forms and write beautiful documents that then sit on a shelf. We often embark on planning before we are clear about which clients we serve and what outcomes we hope to help them achieve. Planning undertaken in the absence of a clear understanding of desired outcomes often deteriorates into discussions of organizational climate and process—of how to make things better for staff, not necessarily for clients and community. The purpose of this chapter is to show how results-oriented management can lead to effective practice. We will outline the steps of an effective planning process, then show some of the common pitfalls of planning in human services and how results-oriented management can make a difference.

Planning is the process by which an agency sets its service priorities and desired levels of achievement for a specified period of time. It is often closely linked with budgeting, the process by which resources are allocated to meet those levels of achievement. Planning is not predicting the environment—that is forecasting, and good planning usually follows forecasting. We should assume that when an agency begins to set service objectives for a year or a quarter, it has already scanned its environment and understands the factors outside the agency that will influence its work.

Planning is not the decision about which clients to serve. That is strategy formulation, and for the time being we will assume the agency has a strategy—namely, a statement of what services it provides, for what clients, and for what purposes. Adapting that statement to a changing environment is the challenge of strategic thinking (the subject of Chapter Nine). Before an agency can do any effective planning, it must understand its strategy.

Planning is not the choice of what client outcomes agency services ought to achieve. The identification of outcomes follows directly from the articulation of strategy, and results-oriented management clearly involves identifying outcomes before beginning any planning. Likewise, planning is not the identification of critical success variables, for results-oriented management also requires the leader to set the agency's critical success variables before planning begins.

Finally, planning is not telling staff what to do. It is a process by which the professionals in your agency reach agreement on agency goals and objectives. It demands discussion, negotiation, and frank assessment of how your agency's resources can best fulfill its mission. It involves building staff commitment.

Before your agency starts planning, I recommend that you complete what I call a client/service matrix. Such a matrix identifies outcomes and critical success variables for every client group your agency serves. Each group with unique demands should be entered separately. For example, if you expect different outcomes for children in foster care than for adolescents in foster care, there should be separate rows for children and for adolescents in the foster care column. If the outcomes are the same but the critical success variables for children and for adolescents are different, each group still needs a separate row.

Once you understand your client/service mix, you and your staff are ready to plan. Planning involves the following steps:

1. Set goals and objectives.
2. Match expectations and resources.

3.   Set performance standards.
4.   Focus training efforts.

Setting Goals and Objectives: Defining a Level of Achievement

For each client/service combination, you and your staff
should negotiate a desired level of achievement—goals and
objectives—for the time period under consideration. Let us assume
you are planning for a year, since most budget cycles run for a year.
This is the point at which having specified your outcomes and
critical success variables explicitly can greatly simplify planning.
Use the outcomes to identify your goals for the year, and the critical
success variables to specify your service objectives. For example, if
you manage a program serving the chronically mentally ill, your
desired outcome might be that chronic patients live as normal a life
in the community as possible. Your critical success variables might
be (1) that patients discharged from hospitals are released to a
community program and (2) that patients, after their status has been
carefully assessed, complete a transition program that teaches skills
in community living.

With outcomes and critical success variables specified, you
are ready to set goals and objectives for the year. In our example,
your goal might be that 50 percent of the hospitalized patients
return to community alternatives during the year. Your objectives
could be that all patients be discharged from the hospital through
your program and that each of these patients completes the
transition living program.

Making these assessments may be tougher than it seems,
especially with respect to goals. In fact, for some outcomes you may
not be able to articulate a desired level of achievement for the year.
For example, if you are leading an adolescent pregnancy program
(like that discussed in Chapter Four) and your outcome criterion is
no second pregnancy in two years, then the goal for the first year
would be no second pregnancy. But if one of your desired outcomes
is economic self-sufficiency for the mother, then one year may well
be too short a time to set for the desired level of outcome achievement. Take the case of Head Start: if one of your desired outcomes

is adult literacy, then the agency must wait until the child is an adult to achieve it.

If you are unable to achieve your desired outcome in a single period, don't worry. Your goal is to help clients move toward desired outcomes. In many cases, you will be able to set intermediate levels of outcome achievement for the planning period. In Head Start, for example, one could set progressive goals of achievement in reading and writing as participating clients move through school. What is important is that you understand the way the outcome will be achieved over time.

Let us return to the adolescent pregnancy example. We suggested a desired outcome of no second pregnancy within the first year. Assuming you have twenty-four young women in the program, should no second pregnancies within the first year be the desired level of achievement for the program? Maybe, but not necessarily. You need to set realistic goals and objectives, and to do this, you need to know what would be likely to happen in the absence of your program.

Remember the physician discussed in Chapter Four. Suppose that physician aspired to prevent some rare disease and set a goal of having no more than five cases of the disease in the community in the year. That sounds admirable unless you learn that the past twenty years have seen no more than four cases a year. If only four of the twenty-four women in the teen pregnancy program are likely to get pregnant in the absence of the program, no pregnancies would be an admirable and quite possibly appropriate goal; but if past experience suggests that more than half of the twenty-four would conceive, then no pregnancies may be an unrealistic goal. Since your goals and objectives become the standard by which your workers and outsiders measure program effectiveness, you want to be realistic. You also want to challenge the organization to greater productivity, but without engendering staff frustration over wildly unrealistic goals.

Matching Expectations and Resources

At the outset of planning, you need a general idea of the level of resources that will be available to you during the year. Granted, you may not know exactly how much new money you will get from the legislature or a fund-raising campaign, but you should make a reasonable estimate. If you are not honest with your agency about resources, you may be setting yourself up for a fall. The leader who encourages agency staff to set whatever performance expectations they want will cause major disappointment if he or she must later say, "Sorry—you can only have a third that much."

A better plan is to provide some resource guidelines when planning begins. You try to set goals and objectives that are roughly within those guidelines. If not, then clear and explicit outcomes and critical success variables should provide the backup information essential for decision making. For instance, if additional resources can be acquired—the topic of the next chapter—then the explicitly stated outcomes and critical success variables will aid in preparing and presenting the case for those additional resources. If such resources are not available, the statement of outcomes and critical success variables will help you set priorities and decide where to cut service aspirations. Unfortunately, there are no magic formulas to tell you how and where to cut. You must judge where cuts in activity will have the least impact on the outcomes that are most important to you and your agency. You would not be a leader if you lacked such judgment.

If you have trouble making such decisions, this is where specifying outcomes and critical success variables can help. For each outcome identified, list the level of achievement you desire for the planning period. Rate all the goals from 1 to 10, with 10 the assessment for the goal of greatest importance to achieving the agency's mission. It is okay to have more than one goal you rated 10. Once the rating is done, you will be able to look at the impact of various budget allocations on the competing goals. And once you have identified your desired achievement level, the budgetary implications of achieving various outcome objectives will be clear. This information, along with your rating, can lead to prudent choices.

For example, assume that you have only two outcomes of concern with the adolescent pregnancy program discussed earlier. First, you want no second pregnancies in two years. Second, you want mothers to have an adequate level of literacy in their adult lives. Your goals for the coming year are to prevent second pregnancies for all first-time mothers and to help all mothers to master ninth-grade skills in reading and writing. The objective in the first case is to make sure that all first-time mothers complete a family planning course; in the second, that all mothers who are in school complete a special tutorial you have prepared.

You know your budget is not sufficient to meet both goals completely. The problem is payment for transportation and day care. You see two choices. One budget alternative will allow 60 percent achievement on the family planning goal and 50 percent achievement on education. Another allocation might give you an 80 percent achievement on family planning but only 30 percent on education. Which budget do you choose? If you rated achievement on family planning at 9 on your scale of value and education at 5, then you should go with the second budget. It is worth more, as shown, in the table that follows. This table in essence shows how to produce a net achievement score (the result of multiplying the level of achievement by the basic value of outcome) that reflects the impact of the achievement on your agency mission. You want to manage for the greatest outcome, and the table suggests that the second budget will give a slightly higher return for your investment of resources.

Budget Impact Comparisons

	Achievement	×	Value	=	Impact
Budget 1					
Family Planning	.60		9		5.4
Education	.50		5		2.5
				Total	7.9
Budget 2					
Family Planning	.80		9		7.2
Education	.30		5		1.5
				Total	8.7

Admittedly, this is a simple approach. In reality, you may face program planning issues that do not lend themselves to this kind of arithmetic. For example, you may have to provide service to everyone or to no one, with no way to provide service to only some. Should you ever need a more complex procedure, refer to Raiffa (1968), on whose approach to decision analysis this example is based, and to Keeney and Raiffa (1976), who deal with making choices among programs with complex, conflicting objectives. You might also want to refer to Hatry, Blair, Fisk, and Kimmel (1976), who provide a very practical approach to program analysis in public agencies, or to Thompson (1980), who offers a useful approach to cost-benefit analysis in program evaluation. While my approach does not resolve the tough issues dealt with in those more detailed references, it brings them into focus so you can think about them during the planning process.

Setting Performance Standards

Once you have a set of goals and objectives, you should proceed to translate them into clear performance standards for work units and individuals. But first, a note about the planning process. As a leader, you should aim for a high degree of staff investment in whatever goals you set for the agency. As is adequately documented elsewhere, employees have a higher level of investment in goals they set for themselves than in goals imposed on them.

This chapter and Chapter Four describe a way of thinking that, as should be obvious by now, should not and cannot be for the leader alone. The leader must engage staff in the six steps of results-oriented management if there is to be maximum payoff. For you to set goals in which staff can be highly invested, the staff must have first crack at identifying clients and outcomes for the services they operate. Review and negotiate this list with them. Then provide them with what I call the parameters for planning, the resource and policy boundaries within which they will plan. At this point, you should be quite candid about your perceptions of problems or opportunities in their program areas. They then need the chance to propose a set of service goals for the work unit for the year. That, too, should be negotiated. You need not accept their proposals at face value, but then you must explain clearly why your expectations differ.

With these negotiations complete, give individuals the oportunity to propose a set of personal performance standards for the work period. This, too, should be negotiated, but between the staff member and the supervisor responsible for the work unit. Although the resulting agreement need not be called a performance contract, it will in essence be one. If, as I suggest, the principal functions for which individual performance standards are being set up are expressed in terms of critical success variables, then those contracts will in effect translate your program into very real, achievable performance milestones for every member of your organization.

You might want to insist that individual standards be set up for quarterly performance goals. Lee Iacocca (1984) does this with his managers, and his logic is persuasive. He suggests that a year is too long a period for individual performance goals. Goals can be forgotten if they are reviewed only annually, and they may well drift away from reality in an agency that is changing fast. On the other hand, a month is too short a period; there is not enough time to get things done. A quarter is an appropriate time period for monitoring and reassessing individual performance, and such reassessment really has to be driven by the agency planning process.

Focusing Training Efforts

Training is seldom considered part of planning. When agencies and managers discuss resource allocation, the discussion almost always centers around budgets. Yet if you examine almost any human services budget, you will find that some 80 percent of it goes for salaries and benefits—for people. Thus, if the human services leader wants to focus agency resources on the goals and objectives derived from an assessment of outcomes and critical success variables, he or she must be able to direct the work of those people. One way to do this, of course, is to set performance goals. But the direction of training is also critical. Too often, training is set up around the wrong factors. It is treated as a staff benefit rather than a management tool, and its content is left to the discretion of individuals who do not understand the organization's overall mission. Training is the first area to be cut when budgets are tight. Locating the training program at a local resort may become more important than content.

This is all wrong, for the quality of human services depends inexorably on the quality of the contact between individual caregiver and client. The best objectives in the world will go down the drain unless the worker has the skills to deliver the service as designed, to implement the critical success variables. For example, take the cases of Corey Greer (Chapter One) and Dwayne Harrington (Chapter Four). In both instances, workers either misunderstood the roles they were to play, lacked the required skills, or understood too little about child development to diagnose the situation accurately once it was presented to them. In both cases, the prevailing agency attitude was to work at the convenience of the staff, not to the benefit of the client.

Training is the way a leader attacks such problems. An annual training plan is not a frill; it is an essential tool for the effective leader. It allows the leader to channel human energy toward desired outcomes by ensuring the successful delivery of critical agency services. It allows the leader to develop awareness of the roles, skills, knowledge, and attitudes necessary to achieving desired client outcomes. Then the manager has the basis for an extensive training effort.

First, there is guidance for preservice training. For caregivers, supervisors, and managers, such preservice training ought to be geared to the entries in the client/service matrix for the outcomes and critical success variables over which they have authority. Continuing inservice training ought to be focused on changes in those roles, skills, areas of knowledge, and attitudes brought about by changes in clients, outcomes, and critical success variables.

As an example, assume you are designing a training program for the adolescent pregnancy program discussed earlier. One outcome for that program is competent parenting on the part of the mothers, with a corresponding critical success variable of completion of a parenting course. To achieve this outcome, the worker must play the role of teacher/counselor; must have knowledge of parenting skills, particularly how single parents can successfully fill this role; must understand adolescent development, to be effective in teaching parenting skills; must know the environment in which the teen mother will raise her children; and must have counseling skill and exhibit an attitude of confidence in the teen parent. Other outcomes and their corresponding critical success variables will demand other knowledge, skills, and attitudes. Together, these competencies form the core of preservice and inservice training for workers. Supervisors and managers will require additional training relevant to teaching, coaching, monitoring, and encouraging effective performance in the roles identified for the process suggested here.

It is a myth that the kind of training described here is going to be expensive. The Commonwealth of Massachusetts has a statewide training center that offers such preservice training, for all employees. It combines expert training in fields relevant to social services with instruction in the specifics of department policy and provides a selection of inservice courses on new developments in these fields and on new policies and practices. Its 1986 budget was approximately $3 million.

The Case for Caution

If this kind of planning sounds too simple—and too much like what you are already doing—consider the case of an agency we shall call the Children's Center. That agency had a stated mission of becoming a comprehensive regional child welfare resource for children, youth, and families. It was an agency with a long tradition, having been started in the mid-nineteenth century by a religious order as a home for orphans. Over the years the importance of its residential facility had been reduced until, in the late 1960s, that facility had closed. The Children's Center now specialized in counseling services, day treatment, and day-care services.

To a large extent, the Children's Center was ahead of other voluntary agencies in its state. Other agencies were embroiled in sometimes bitter negotiations with the state over reimbursement rates for residential services—services the state was increasingly reluctant to purchase. For the voluntary agencies, reimbursement had become a survival issue, and the Children's Center was spared the agony of the rate battles. Consequently, its relationship with the state was better than that of other service agencies.

Planning was extremely important for the Children's Center. Competition for day-care dollars was growing. Much of the state's support for day care was funded by Social Security Services Grant monies, and the center was rightfully worried about the survival of those funds in the Gramm-Rudman-Hollings era. In-home services for the elderly were increasingly contracted to private, for-profit providers who argued that they could provide high-quality services for lower cost than their voluntary counterparts. Staff reported that the children and youth referred by the state were generally older and more troubled than in the past. It was critical for the Children's Center to engage in careful, productive planning.

The center outlined a planning process of seven steps. First, management would define the agency's mission. Second, data would be gathered on problems and resources. Third, service objectives would be set. Fourth, specific program plans to reach the objectives would be drawn up. Fifth, a budget would be drafted. Sixth, the budget would be reviewed and modified. Seventh, a balanced budget would be adopted.

With the mission of the agency defined as becoming a comprehensive child welfare agency, the Children's Center went to work. It gathered general data about trends in child welfare and family life in its state. It undertook a major survey of organizational climate, which showed that many staff were unhappy with the way management decisions were made and wanted to become more involved in setting policy. Senior managers articulated a set of goals that included establishing a sound financial base, maintaining quality, using buildings more efficiently, becoming a community leader, supporting professionalism among staff, and building the board of trustees.

Against this background, each program area set objectives for the year. In day treatment, for example, goals were to attract and retain qualified staff, extend clinical services, provide adequate supervision, and provide incentives and recognition for staff. Objectives for the year were to upgrade base salaries, add two new positions, and increase staff levels at all facilities.

When all the program objectives were reviewed by the senior managers, enormous frustration resulted. The budgetary needs of the various programs vastly exceeded available resources, and there was no way to make comparisons and evaluate tradeoffs. More important, the planning process did not answer many of the managers' key questions about how the center's services would secure its niche in the broader network of service agencies. It was not clear how the center would answer its critics and competitors. It appeared to some that the agency plan was being developed more for the convenience of staff than to provide quality services for clients.

What went wrong? On the surface, the planning process for the Children's Center seems to make sense. In fact, it seems remarkably like the one proposed here. Indeed, the difference between what we have proposed and what the Children's Center did is not so much in the process as in the starting point. The Children's Center began its planning process without a clear focus on its clients and the outcomes it hoped to help them achieve. It had only a general sense of its mission and of the problems that children and families brought to the agency. Even though many staff undoubtedly knew their clients' problems in detail, those problems did not drive the planning process. As in many agencies, the most detailed data available to the Children's Center were those on staff attitudes and preferences. As a result, the noteworthy aspirations for high-quality services were going to be realized by increasing staff comfort and pay. While both those changes might have enhanced services, the need for specific improvements in client outcomes was not what put them into the plan.

For the Children's Center's planning process to have answered the managers' questions, the center needed more focus at the outset. It needed a statement of its mission, one that identified its intended clients and intended services. Even a broad statement that the center aspired "to provide nonresidential treatment services to children and families at risk of abuse and neglect" would have been a better starting point. From there, each service area could have identified its intended clients and problems. Then it could have articulated its hoped-for outcomes and the corresponding critical success variables. The process of setting goals and objectives and preparing budget proposals would then have made more sense and enabled senior managers to make the difficult but necessary choices.

A Simple Example

Let's suppose that the Children's Center had articulated exactly the mission just stated and that we are responsible for preparing a rough plan for day care. We have been told to plan within a budget no larger than 10 percent more than currently allotted.

Our primary clients are children two to four years of age. They come from families who have committed acts of abuse or neglect or are at risk of doing so. In screening children for admission, priority is given to: children from families with marginal incomes, children from households headed by single parents, and children referred from the state. However, the center has tried to limit these categories to no more than one-third of the caseload so as not to become too dependent on state funding. We hope that as a result of day care each child will enjoy normal mental, physical, and social development during the two years of care. We also expect that their families will be strengthened and that family stress will be reduced as a result of their children's being involved in care.

With these outcomes in mind, we suggest the following critical success variables. First, to ensure normal mental development, we must have a carefully designed learning program. For physical growth, we need a recreational program and nutritionally balanced lunch and snack plan; for social development, a regimen of play activities that balances individual and group work. To strengthen families, it is critical to have family involvement in key activities that reflect the child's progress in each of the mental, physical, and social maturation areas.

Despite the seeming simplicity of this setup, it unleashes considerable power in planning. For each outcome level, we can set goals for the year: the children will achieve certain average levels of knowledge, physical growth, and social skill. To help them reach those levels, we know we will have to supply particular teaching and nurturing activities, including a clear schedule of joint activities for families. Our aspirations for these activities become our objectives for the year. Once we have identified what we need to do, we can compare these activities to the resources available to pay for them. If, as often happens, reaching the desired level of achievement would cost more than the agency can expend, we are in a good position to scale back desired achievement levels until resources and objectives are in balance. With this information, the proposal we bring to the Children's Center's management will be rich with detail about service and achievement levels possible in day care. We will have a specific set of objectives for the children. And once the budget is approved, we will be able to ask each of our day-care staff to set personal performance objectives that will help reach the program goals. We can then prepare a detailed training plan focused on achieving our goals and objectives. We should be able to answer all questions, at the outset of the center's planning process.

6

⊗⊗⊗⊗

Managing the Budget

The last chapter discussed the use of clear outcomes and critical success variables in making tough choices when agency objectives cost more to realize than is available. Objectives must be realistic to be useful. But leaders cannot always just cut back on aspirations to match resources. They must also be ready to fight for new resources. In an era of large federal budget deficits and tax-control initiatives at the state and local levels, the ability to win at the budget game, to attract new resources to deserving service aspirations, is a leadership necessity. How to do that is the subject of this chapter.

We begin in the middle, for we assume there is an existing budget and that the leader is already trying to manage that budget. It is important today that leaders be able to manage to maximum advantage their existing resources. This task usually consumes much of their time and deserves our attention.

At the time of writing, Gramm-Rudman-Hollings hovers as a dark cloud over human services funding at the federal level. A number of key sources of social services funding, the Social Services Block Grant, for example, have been targets as Congress has grappled with reducing the federal budget deficit. Simultaneously, many states are coming to grips with various spending limits—property tax lids or rollbacks, limits on the growth of state budgets and work forces and even on the salaries of public executives. Education, transportation, and other public services compete with increasing vigor for a share of a funding pie that is growing only slowly. State budget officials and legislative fiscal staffs are more sophisticated than ever in their analysis of data on spending and activity. There may have been a time when the human services leader could delegate the monitoring and preparation of a budget to an accountant or budget officer. No more. The budget, with all its intergovernmental complications, is the center of a struggle for public support of human services.

The complicated nature of the budget process is not news. Wildavsky (1974) documents that complexity and provides a set of strategies for coping with it, at the federal level at least. While his advice is relevant to human services, it is not specific to them or to the special challenges currently facing human services leaders. Other books, Anthony and Young (1984) among them, deal with mechanics.

This chapter deals with managing the broader flow of resources and with ways that leaders can direct that flow toward outcomes. It examines not just the politics of getting new funding but also how the flow of existing funds must be managed. Indeed, making a case for new funds depends on the leader's ability to demonstrate that existing funds are efficiently used.

Managing Existing Funding Streams

Although constraints abound, a leader has to be able to find flexibility within existing funding streams. In states with a balanced-budget requirement, governors often do not allocate the full amount appropriated by the legislature, to guard against a shortfall in revenue collection. There are usually strict line-item controls on transferring monies from one budget category to another. The budgets for many programs include federal funds that bring with them their own specific eligibility regulations.

How all these constraints interact is illustrated in the following example. You manage a program that provides in-home health care to the elderly. Your most recent budget report shows that your actual expenditures for service are below the levels you projected when you constructed your budget. If these levels of expenditure were to continue for the rest of the fiscal year, you will underspend your budget. It would seem that you have some flexibility here. If current service rates are not fully utilizing budgeted funds, you would appear to have the option to increase service levels or to try to transfer funds from the home health care budget category to a related service, say to nutrition services for the elderly.

In fact, I know a program manager who faced this situation but who had no budget flexibility at all. In this case, while the actual expenditures were below budget projections, the manager knew that state revenue collections were below expected levels. The governor in this state faced a constitutional mandate to balance the budget. To do so, the governor had the power to reduce budget allotments, the amounts that agencies could spend, below the budget levels approved by the legislature. The manager fully expected the governor to reduce the allotment for the health care program. When the allotment was reduced, the actual level of expenditures was in line with the amount of money the manager had available. By watching the broader economic and budget context, this manager was able to avoid a budget error. The manager understood very well that simply comparing expenditures with budgets does not tell the leader where budget flexibility might lie.

Here is another example, in foster care. A manager I know received a budget report at midyear showing actual expenditures below budget by a fair amount. Furthermore, program activity data indicated a steady decline in the number of children in foster care. The agency had devoted considerable effort to developing alternative programs to foster care, and activity data reflected the fact that the programs were having the desired effect. Because there was no reduced allocation process under way or likely in this state at the time, the manager moved quickly to gain approval to use this pool of flexible funds for new purposes. The manager sought to use some of what would otherwise have been unexpended funds to support a modest increase in the reimbursement rates for foster parents. The manager then sought approval to transfer the foster care money into a budget allocation for alternative programs. Both efforts were successful, for several reasons. First, the requests were based on sound analysis of both program and financial data. Second, both requests were consistent with longstanding policy directions of the agency. These directions had strong support from legislative and executive leadership. Third, the manager enjoyed a sound working relationship with the state budget office. The budget officials knew the foster care program, they had received program data on a regular basis, and they were well informed of the success of the alternative programs. Finally, the manager in this case watched the budget closely. The likely surplus was detected early enough in the budget year that necessary budget office approvals could be obtained without putting undue pressure on the budget office.

These two examples illustrate what the successful leader must know:

1. The leader must have regular reports on spending versus budget. The leader should have a spending plan that sets realistic spending expectations for each month of the fiscal year. Monthly reports should then reflect actual spending as compared to this plan.
2. The leader must understand how spending relates to service activity in a fiscal year. For example, reports on child abuse and neglect vary markedly by season of the year. To assume that funds earmarked for care for abused and neglected children will be spent in a steady stream does not reflect the reality of service delivery. In addition, many purchase-of-service contracts suffer a lag in reimbursement at the beginning of the fiscal year. Contracts need to be approved, accounts set up, and so forth. A budget account for such services may show steady under-spending for a year, when in fact it has simply fallen behind in the first month and has yet to catch up.
3. The leader must know where there is flexibility. There is no substitute for understanding the opportunities for flexibility in each funding stream under the leader's control.
4. The leader has to be sensitive to how the broader policy context may affect his or her program. For example, if a crisis has arisen around schools' nonreporting of child abuse, an emphasis on school reporting may follow, meaning that any continued underspending in child-abuse investigation would be inadvisable.
5. The leader must monitor the state of the economy. A downturn

in economic indicators typically suggests that public agencies should plan to underspend, because downturns are often followed by reductions in funding allocations at the state level or hiring and spending restrictions at state or local agencies.

6.   The leader—or a trusted lieutenant—must know the rules of funding transfer, that is, under what conditions and by what process funding from one account or line item might be transferred to another. He or she must know who can or must approve what budget changes and what information is required.

There is more involved here than knowing a set of clearly specified procedures. The rules on budget change constantly. In many cases, the interpretation of a rule can vary significantly from case to case. To know the rules, the leader must know the rule makers. The leader, the agency, and its programs should be familiar to the various fiscal officers and budget officials who must act on a proposed change. Knowing the rule makers means you introduce them to your programs, operating procedures, and outcome and performance standards. It also means developing and using guidelines for program management that reflect the priorities of such officials.

Building up contacts with the rule makers usually is not as difficult as it may seem. It is only time consuming. You have to take the time to get to know them, the nature of their jobs, and their priorities, and to school them in the workings of human services programs, which often means adapting your style of reporting to their preferred way of learning. This frequently means getting information to them in any way and at any time you can. It also means becoming aware of and catering to the priorities of the rule makers' bosses—the governors, legislators, and controllers. That means including regular progress reports on those priorities along with your reports on program results. It means looking for ways to achieve some of those priorities within the areas of your responsibility.

The Missouri Department of Social Services developed a useful management report format in the early 1980s to facilitate such reporting. The format included two pages reporting on each service program in the agency: one page summarizing client activity and one page summarizing budget data. The client activity page showed a graph of client services, typically over a two- to three-year period. It also included supporting data to provide actual numbers of clients served. The graph proved to help busy decision makers spot trends in service demand and distinguish long-term trends from seasonal variations. The budget page provided corresponding graphs and data on spending. Developed initially for agency use, the report eventually became a useful tool for communicating with legislative and budget staff outside the agency.

I am always amazed at the number of executives who have never met the officials who review and act on their budgets and who lack working command of the facts those people need to make decisions. Timely response to their questions, and their being able to associate your face with your name and program, can make the difference. Budget officials advise governors and legislators on difficult tradeoffs among programs with widely varying outcomes and operating styles. Those budget advisers are asked to make judgments about the efficiency and effectiveness of programs they often do not understand, and to the extent they feel comfortable that you as agency leader can provide them with timely and useful information when those tradeoffs must be made, they are more likely to ask you for it.

One key to dealing with the rules and the rule makers is to have an agency budget official who is comfortable with program matters and also enjoys the confidence of the rule makers. Such people are rare, but surprisingly few leaders try to nurture such individuals in their organizations. Budget officers are often closed out of management decisions and program matters, and not consulted about policy decisions until the decisions must be implemented. That is a mistake. Since the budget officer is the person in the organization most likely to know the language of rule making and to have working contact with rule makers, the leader should use that person as a bridge between clients, services, and the budget process.

The importance of using current public funding sources to the maximum, even in novel ways, is illustrated by the case of Title IV-E of the Social Security Act, which provides funding on an entitlement basis to children in foster care who are eligible for Aid to Families with Dependent Children (AFDC). The entitlement is for direct foster care expenses and for the administrative expenses associated with case management. To reclaim the latter, states are required to document the amount of expense through actual studies of foster care case management. With the advent of permanency planning, the federal government, expecting that foster care caseloads would decline markedly, offered states the option of accepting a voluntary ceiling on their Title IV-E payments. Rather than lose funds, states could accept a ceiling based on their most recent experience and then use those funds to pay for new non-foster care programming. States were thereby excused from what was perceived as the onerous task of doing the time-motion studies required to recoup administrative costs. In most states, foster care caseloads have not declined as dramatically as expected. Since those states have usually never done the studies necessary to exploit Title IV-E fully, most of them now receive much less than they could. Missouri estimates, for example, that by not electing to impose the voluntary ceiling, it can recoup some $4 million from Title IV-E, especially since the requirements for the administrative studies have been relaxed.

The Center for the Study of Social Policy (1986) has recommended a number of similar steps for a wide range of entitlement programs. It suggests that Medicaid can be used as a source of funding for counseling and other health-related services. The center suggests that Medicaid could also be used to a greater extent to pay for health, mental health, and some developmental services for eligible children who are in institutions as a result of child abuse and neglect. Medicaid and Medicaid waivers can be utilized to pay for in-home health services for clients including the elderly, the adult mentally retarded, and families at risk of institutional placement of a child. Energy assistance options of the Aid to Families with Dependent Children program can be used to help provide food, clothing, and housing. Some states have expanded the range of emergency situations to include child abuse and neglect situations, thereby using this program to help promote family preservation.

A second set of examples illustrates the use of federal policies to help draw more private dollars into support for children. Following the lead of Wisconsin, many states have revised their laws on child support. Wisconsin pioneered in mandated payment schedules and using paycheck deductions to make sure child support was actually paid. When Wisconsin began this effort, the national average for child support payments was a mere 30 percent of what the courts awarded. In many cases, states were left to fill the gap through public assistance. With legislatively mandated payment schedules and collection procedures, more parental dollars can flow into the support of children at risk. Florida and other states have recently taken another step in this direction by enacting statutes allowing court-awarded child support to help pay for treatment of status offenders, particularly for those children who are "throwaways" (that is, children whose parents surrender them to the state for care).

A more direct approach to generating private dollars for human services is under way at the School of Social Work at the University of Texas, Austin. That school has embarked on an effort to persuade private employers to spend more money on an array of employee assistance programs, including marriage and substance abuse counseling and day care. Their argument is not that these services are good for the community, although they undoubtedly are. They argue that such expenditures are in the best interests of the individual business enterprise. The school's data show that absenteeism and poor productivity resulting from child care responsibilities, family problems, and substance abuse more than warrant the increased subsidy of employee assistance.

These examples suggest that there is no reason to despair in times of tight public budgets. There are opportunities for better utilization of existing intergovernmental and private funding streams, and leaders should pursue them.

Going for New Money

This discussion should not be taken to imply that all a leader need do is manage existing funding creatively. Such sources may be inadequate, and a leader must be able to generate additional monies. In the public arena that means generating public support for a program and a proposal, not easy at any time, particularly in this time of tax and expenditure limits. How can public support be marshaled and focused on specific proposals for new resources for human services?

First, we must recognize that allocations of public resources are political decisions. Politicans, governors, and legislators prefer to deliver programs that pay off for their constituents. The obvious challenge to generating more support for human services is to submit budget proposals that show promise of helping elected officials earn the confidence, and eventually the votes, of the public.

It would be naive to believe that all elected officials think alike or even share the same frame of mind about their responsibility to the public. Still, it is probably true that elected officials, particularly political executives, come into office with a vague sense of obligation to the electorate. If, as former North Carolina Governor Jim Hunt once said, a gubernatorial election is the process of writing a contract between a governor and the people, then governors typically have a program and a purpose and, in fact, are looking for ways to translate that program into specific proposals that have a chance at being approved by a legislature.

The task for the leader seeking new public funds is to develop a proposal that helps the political executive win. That means creating a proposal that not only responds to the priorities of the agency but also fits into the gubernatorial program. Further, the proposal must help the governor implement the program relatively quickly and effectively, to avoid any political embarrassment. The art of budget strategy, then, is the art of balancing internal needs with political reality. The leader is expected to select and propose those new programs that will both advance his agency's mission and fulfill the political agenda set by the executive and legislative branches.

While such judgment is not subject to rigid formula, there is a way to sharpen it. Barrett Toan, drawing on a concept introduced by Robert Reich at the John F. Kennedy School of Government, suggests that leaders structure their initial budget thinking around a *strategic audit*. The leader uses the strategic audit to assess internal and external agency momentum and design programs that make the most of both. The leader needs to assess the agency's strengths and weaknesses on the one hand, and his or her political strengths and weaknesses on the other. Programs that draw on both sets of strengths are prime candidates for new resources.

Completing a strategic audit should be relatively simple and straightforward. The first step is to assess program momentum inside the agency, that is, the agency's relative strengths and weaknesses in providing its various services. On a strategic audit chart, the areas of momentum would be entered on the plus side, and areas of weakness on the minus side. Which programs are of high quality? Which programs need development? The leader needs to understand staff preferences and skills. What program initiatives are being developed inside the agency? What directions would the staff pursue on their own?

For example, imagine a child welfare agency that has a strong unit investigating abuse and neglect and whose investigative workers have noted an increasing number of sexual abuse cases. A natural development in such a unit would be a special focus on sexual abuse. That agency would have internal momentum in the direction of sexual abuse investigation.

Here's a second example. Assume that your foster care unit has for some time been concerned with a growing number of physically handicapped children. The unit has explored options for a specialized category of foster homes for such children and has begun to develop budget projections for funding such homes. There is momentum in the direction of serving handicapped children.

In addition to assessing strengths, you need to be honest about areas of weakness, areas in which there is a lack of internal momentum. If your abuse and neglect unit were having difficulty, if you had not, say, been able to meet your objectives in investigating abuse cases, then you would lack the momentum to specialize in investigating sexual abuse.

Once you have assessed internal momentum, you need to turn your attention to developments outside the agency. What do your constituents desire? In what directions are other social services agencies moving? What are the top political priorities of relevant elected officials? For example, if your governor were elected with a strong promise to provide early childhood education services and had several initiatives in that direction under way in other agencies, then there is external momentum in the direction of early childhood programs. If your foster care providers have organized and are ready to lobby the legislature on behalf of higher rates, that has momentum. On the other hand, if private day-care providers have petitioned the legislature to exempt them from licensing standards, then there is no momentum toward higher standards. Similarly, if your governor were elected on a promise of holding the line on state spending, there is little outside momentum toward higher expenditures in big-ticket items such as income support.

Once you have assessed external momentum, you would list the areas with momentum on the plus side and areas of controversy or opposition on the minus side. Then you would identify programs that are consistent with the plus side internally and externally. Programs for which there exists strong internal and outside support are natural candidates for new funds. Those are the programs the agency can develop and implement successfully and that will attract the political support needed for enactment.

Here's an example. An executive with a budget dilemma has listed the following needs:

- Raising salaries of child-protection workers, $12 million
- Raising AFDC payments to the state standard, $250–300 million
- Doubling the number of state-subsidized day-care slots, $50 million
- Developing a worker-training program, $3–5 million
- Extending intensive crisis counseling to families at risk, $5 million
- Automation of casework records, $3–4 million

The executive's challenge is to package these needs into a budget recommendation that the governor might propose to the legislature. Internally, assume the leader has several established programs with proven track records, including a small intensive crisis counseling service that has been documented to prevent out-of-home placement in some 80 percent of the cases in which it is used. The policy group's just-completed study of increasing poverty in the state has produced startling evidence of the effects of poverty on children and families. The personnel office has just completed a study showing that worker salaries are lower than in neighboring states and that low salaries are contributing to extraordinarily high staff turnover.

When this leader has completed the strategic audit, he or she would place those programs with good track records on the plus side—in particular, the intensive crisis counseling program, which is likely to show momentum, since it is a small program that has proven effective but has room to grow. There would also be momentum toward salary adjustment and new initiatives on poverty, since agency staff have begun to identify and develop programs to deal with problems in those areas.

On the external side, the leader is faced with a suspicious, if not hostile, public and press. The department has been the subject of a series of press investigations, and the press and the legislature consistently cite a problem of poor management. The press coverage of child abuse cases has raised public awareness. The governor, who has been helpful on children's issues, has been giving more attention to education. There are well-organized constituency groups and vocal advocacy groups, who are also suspicious of the department but who typically take the side of the workers in arguing for higher pay, more training, and greater professionalism. Several of the constituency groups are well connected to key legislators. They have agreed that better salaries and training are needed. The state is fiscally conservative. It has no income tax, and large communities of retirees consistently vote to keep taxes low. Revenues grow at a steady but single-digit rate. Rapid population growth creates considerable demand for other services, especially in transportation and education.

Faced with this external situation, the leader would enter salary and training on the plus side of the strategic audit (there is outside interest in these issues), along with management initiatives and new quality-assurance mechanisms (also a matter of outside concern). On the minus side would be placed any major new spending initiative, given the interests of the governor, the competition for funds, and the reluctance to increase taxes. The message is that any major spending initiative must be very well developed and have a strong, unified constituency if it is to succeed.

Our audit suggests internal and external momentum toward consensus on salaries and training, but no general support for

major new spending. In this example, the strategic audit indicates
that the leader should press for higher salaries, more training, and
selective program increases. Internally, recent department initiatives argue for doing something about these issues, and there is
public support for them. Increases in public assistance, which are
also very much needed, have internal support but, considering
the magnitude of the need, insufficient outside momentum. On the
other hand, even though some interest groups and members of the
legislature are clamoring for more integration of services and for
program innovation, such proposals have little momentum inside,
where staff have not done much background work on them. Only
in a few selected areas could the leader be sure the agency is ready
to implement program expansion.

Leaders are not constrained to press only for programs that
already have internal and external strength. Suppose that the leader
in the previous example really did want to press for funding for
income maintenance, because of the great need of the children and
families. That program has insufficient internal and external
support to be a candidate for immediate funding. So the leader's
challenge is clear: he or she must build support for the idea inside
and outside the agency. Inside, the leader must develop staff
capabilities so an effective program can be implemented. Externally, the leader must forcefully communicate to the public the
extent of the need, and must package income assistance in ways that
relate to the broader priorities of elected officials. In California last
year, for instance, advocates for public assistance recognized and
took advantage of such an opportunity when they joined in a
coalition to create the dramatic new work-assistance program called
GAIN. They were able to press their concern about adequate levels
of financial assistance on legislators, who were concerned about the
lack of incentives for self-sufficiency built into the existing public
assistance system. Together they designed a program that combined
higher levels of financial assistance with job-training, day-care, and
job-seeking assistance. The combination was powerful. The
internal momentum toward providing more resources to the needy
joined the external momentum to help recipients develop job skills
and find employment.

Budgeting: An Ongoing, Multilevel Game

Implicit in the preceding discussion is the notion that if leaders want new funds, they must improve their ability to demonstrate that existing funds are being spent responsibly. They want only those new funds that can be translated quickly into effective services. To get new funds or to transfer existing funds requires gaining the confidence of fiscal staff and elected officials, who may not understand the program or funding streams, or may not even sympathize with agency clients. Leaders must balance effective internal management with effective external advocacy.

This suggests that obtaining new funds is not far removed from managing existing funds to full benefit. Persuading the budget officer today that a transfer is needed for training may be the first step in justifying the case for more training money next year. The legislative committee that suspects that last year's budget was misspent is not going to be eager to up the ante for next year. And the wise governor will not ask that it do so.

Barrett Toan has said that preparing a proposal for new funding is like preparing the budget for the thirteenth month of the current year. Proposals for new programs should flow from the direction implicit in current activity. Therefore, planning for future budgets begins with managing existing budgets in ways that clarify the vision and purpose of the department. When Toan worked in Missouri for Governor Christopher Bond, they made an effective team for human services in large part because they saw budgeting as a continuing process. They understood that budget management was closely linked to new program development. They tried to lay out a few themes in human services early in the term, and then managed existing and new funding streams consistently according to those themes. They developed a momentum that derived initially from the marriage of dramatic needs of Missouri children with the governor's genuine concern for children.

Toan and Bond understood that the budget process has in reality three interrelated parts. First, it involves management of public funds, that is, allocating, spending, and accounting for funds in a manner consistent with publicly supported goals. Ideally, public dollars flow, via the budget process, to areas of greatest public demand, and leaders have a responsibility to see that they do.

But budgeting is also a matter of program management and policy development. How resources are allocated determines the relative emphases among programs and services. Those emphases, in turn, generate expectations among staff and public about service goals and priorities. That is public policy. When leaders articulate one vision but allocate their resources to another, confusion results. Witness the policy stalemate in states that have said they believe in community service for the mentally ill but have left their money in institutions.

Finally, budgeting is political. It involves building a consensus among program constituents, and it means keeping constituents informed so they can share in the task of advocacy. It demands the exercise of judgment and trying to help clients, agency, constituents, and elected officials all "win" at the same time.

The leader has responsibilities at each stage of each level of the budget process. As the budget is developed, presented or sold, enacted by elected officials, and implemented by staff, the leader must balance resource management, program and policy development, and political tasks. Those responsibilities are summarized in three themes: (1) In resource management, the leader must strive to direct money to those areas in which investment will probably achieve important client outcomes. (2) In policy and program development, budget evolution must follow evolving community and client expectations. (3) In coalition management, the leader must both teach and learn, both educate constituents and find ways to incorporate their priorities into his or her own.

To a certain extent, each of these levels of responsibility has already been dealt with in the development of results-oriented management. Clarity of purpose and client-focused program objectives make each of these tasks easier. However, there is still much to say about the leader's role in resource management, policy and program management, and coalition management. The next four chapters will address these areas. Chapter Seven discusses the leader's role in designing the monitoring systems needed to ensure that resources flow to areas of highest impact. Chapter Eight shows how and why results-oriented management can focus the activities of a service agency. Chapter Nine talks about strategic thinking, a way to keep program direction consistent with community and client needs. Chapter Ten discusses how to create climates for change—building external support for issues that are critical for your clients.

7

❦❦❦

Monitoring and Evaluating
Key Measures of Success

The last chapter suggested that accurate information on program activity was critical to the budget process, and earlier chapters recommended monitoring as one important way leaders can influence their agencies' activities. As Jack Dempsey, long-time head of social services in Michigan, is reported to have said, what gets monitored gets done.

Ironically, there is already so much monitoring and evaluating under way in human services that information systems are overloaded. Frustrated leaders receive excessive amounts of data, in reports that are poorly formatted and nearly always late. Not only do managers not use the reports, they criticize those responsible for creating them. The agencies with the largest, most complex data collection and storage facilities often have the poorest-quality monitoring.

The situation with evaluation is not much better. In Florida, for example, evaluation studies are undertaken only in response to crisis. As a result, many evaluations cover only service delivery—who did what, for whom, and when—but tell senior managers little about whether the programs are achieving intended outcomes or are worth the money they cost. Seldom are program evaluations used as a strategy to test assumptions about service delivery or client needs and thereby to learn how to improve program effectiveness.

The impressive literature on monitoring and evaluation falls into roughly three categories. The first group includes evaluation techniques, for example, the classic works by Weiss (1972), Campbell and Stanley (1966), and Cook and Campbell (1979), which are handy guides to the use of experiments and quasiexperiments in evaluation. The second group covers evaluation in management decision making. Hatry, Winnie, and Fisk (1981) and Anderson and Ball (1978) are typical examples. Those references specific to human services include Schainblatt (1977) and Schainblatt and Hatry (1979) (monitoring outcomes in mental health); Carter (1983) and Koss and others (1979) (monitoring outcomes in social services); Theobold (1985) and Attkisson, Hargreaves, Horowitz, and Sorenson (1978) (evaluation in human services). The third category includes works on cost/benefit analysis, such as Mishan's (1976) classic work and Thompson (1980). Even though many of these studies are recent and such techniques are increasingly available, new tools are being underutilized.

The present chapter is intended to help resolve this dilemma. It is not, however, about evaluation techniques, for which the references just cited are better sources. It is also not about the design of automated data management systems. This chapter tells leaders how to use monitoring and evaluation to reinforce their strategies for agency effectiveness and to keep the agency's vision clear and its programs on target.

Leaders often see monitoring and evaluation as so complex that they delegate those tasks to specialists, information systems experts, or statisticians. The results, often technically precise, are practically irrelevant and so are ignored. But monitoring and evaluation need to be designed by the leader in a way that reinforces the agency's mission. This job can be made manageable for the leader through the clarification of outcomes and critical success variables.

A Few Definitions

To avoid any confusion over exactly what a monitoring system or a program evaluation ought to show, let me first clarify the ideas of *program effectiveness* and *program efficiency*. Human services leaders want to know whether their program or service is effective. Is the program doing what it is supposed to do? That is,

(1) is it having its intended effect on its intended clients? And (2) is it having any other effects on other clients or on the community at large? For instance, (1) does a child abuse and neglect investigation program keep its children safe? And (2) does it accurately detect abuse and neglect without unduly disrupting family life?

Human services leaders are also interested in program efficiency. Is the program or service making the best use of available resources? Are there perhaps more efficient ways to organize or move people and equipment, to save time and money? Is there another, less expensive way to provide the same level of client outcome? For instance, can the abuse and neglect reporting system be streamlined to cut the time and staff effort involved without putting children or families at additional risk?

If leaders are sure their programs are both effective and efficient and have evidence to persuade others that this is so, then they can be sure their vision is being realized and their blueprint for action is the right one. In other words, the agency must be generating as much outcome as possible from its available resources.

Effectiveness and efficiency are definitely hard to monitor in human services. There is no equivalent to the private-sector indicator of profit which captures so much about both effectiveness and efficiency. In most cases, human services cannot be packaged and sold to clients in a way that allows profit to reflect either customer satisfaction or operating productivity. This is because: outcomes are often far removed in time from the delivery of a service; there are multiple constituencies, several clients affected by the same service encounter, and a broader community that pays for the services delivered to others; many outcomes are intangible, and thus hard to measure and even more difficult to put a monetary value on. As a consequence, we usually get one of two extremes in monitoring and evaluation: (a) the collection of too many data, making the system cumbersome and unworkable, or (b) the use of the single, exceptional case as a basis for making decisions.

Having a clearer understanding of effectiveness and efficiency, we can now define monitoring and evaluation in ways that help avoid these pitfalls. *Evaluation* is the formal comparison of actual with intended results. It assesses both effectiveness and efficiency, but emphasizes effectiveness, in terms of whether or not an activity generates acceptable outcomes. To allow enough time for outcomes to become clear, program evaluations are typically done every several years.

Monitoring, on the other hand, involves regular and more frequent reports to managers and leaders about program activity, emphasizing efficiency and critical success variables. Thus, we can contrast monitoring—that is, the tracking of performance on critical success variables—with evaluation—that is, the comparing of outcomes achieved with outcomes desired, to gauge whether agency activity has had its intended effect. Good monitoring makes evaluation much easier, and for this reason we will discuss monitoring first.

Monitoring

Let us begin with an example, the adolescent pregnancy program discussed in earlier chapters. Suppose the program has been in operation for a month or two. What would you want to know? If you were to make a list of questions, it would probably be rather lengthy. How many mothers are enrolled? With how many babies? How many fathers are known and involved? How many of the mothers are in school? What is the health status of the mothers and the infants? What are the attitudes of the parents? What are we doing with respect to birth control information? Do we have effective links with the health and social services departments? And so on. And every month the list will get longer. Next month, a school board member will call and ask about a particular child. Embarrassed when we do not know the answer, we will send out a memo asking that information be provided on every child from now on. The next month, the county manager questions why we bought a certain piece of equipment when another was on contract. So we ask for regular reports on planned and actual equipment purchases. And this is how our monitoring system grows. Do we really need to know the answers to all those questions? No. We only clog the system with information and frustrate those who now must spend more time completing our reports than helping adolescent mothers.

It need not turn out this way. For example, with the

adolescent pregnancy program, we already know what clients we serve, what outcomes we expect, and what the critical program activities are. We should have been able to design an effective monitoring system with little trouble at the outset of program operation. Regular reporting on critical success variables would then help us monitor for effectiveness; concise expenditure reports would provide basic data on efficiency. If necessary, we can request other reports on special program goals that, for operating or political reasons, warrant close monitoring—the implementation of birth control policies, for example. Thus, once we have identified critical success variables, the skeleton of our monitoring system is present.

Critical Success Variables and Program Effectiveness

In Chapter Five, it was suggested that you begin your planning by constructing a client/service matrix that shows expected outcomes for each client group served by a program. You then identify a set of critical success variables for each service. Design of the monitoring system should take off from there. For example, that there should be no second pregnancies was an intended outcome of the adolescent pregnancy program; the corresponding critical success variable was that every mother should complete a course in family planning. It is easy to see, given this, that participation in the family planning program should be monitored. Critical success variables for client health, particularly for child health, can also be translated easily into monitoring terms. For example, one of our child health outcomes was that infants develop at a normal pace during their first two years, and its corresponding critical success variable was that each child should participate in a screening program and receive normal infant inoculations. So, to ensure healthy children, we want to monitor both participation in the screening program and inoculation records, which is easy enough to do.

When monitoring critical success variables, you want to compare them with the expected levels that were set in the planning process. For example, the critical variable in child abuse investigation, that the agency see every child within twenty-four hours of a report, might reasonably be expected to be achieved 95 percent of the time, and so you monitor for 95 percent compliance.

The larger the agency or program, the more important it becomes to express such comparisons graphically, for ease of interpretation. For example, for the program that investigates child abuse and neglect, a monthly report might include a bar graph that compares the performance of each investigation unit with the expected 95 percent rate: separate bars would represent the percentage of abuse cases seen by each unit; a horizontal line across the bars would show the 95 percent standard. Then you could quickly and easily see which units were at, above, or below standard.

Budgets and Program Efficiency

Monthly budget reports that track actual versus expected expenditures for the full set of funding streams for your programs are a necessary beginning for monitoring efficiency. However, this may be insufficient. For example, your budget might include line items that cross program categories, such as "personnel," which might cover people who work on different programs even though it is listed as a single budget item. Also, since it is not unusual for salaries and wages to constitute as much as 80 percent of expenditures, actual versus expected expenditures on personnel may be a poor measure of efficiency.

In such a case, you may need a report on a few key indicators of efficiency. Many agencies caseload data, although doing so invites gamesmanship in case management. Witness the large metropolitan office that refused to close child protective cases for fear of losing staff positions, and whose active caseload grew so large as a result that it became unmanageable.

Work process standards may be better indicators of efficiency. For example, time limits for handling particular types of casework, such as investigating a report of abuse, may be more effective. Even then, you need to be cautious. Efficiency measures without quality control (see the next section) invite workers to shortchange clients in counterproductive ways. In addition, efficiency measures have an extraordinary way of cluttering up the monitoring system. They should be used only when the information they generate can lead to action. In other words, monitor only what you can change. (If you really cannot change caseload levels, don't monitor them.)

I am dubious about efficiency measures that are not also critical success variables. I recommend that leaders monitor for results—that is, monitor critical success variables—and give their workers latitude with respect to process. Left on their own, workers are probably better than their managers at figuring out how to make their time and effort go further. Once leaders get into time-and-motion study, their clarity of vision disappears.

A Note on Quality Control

Quality of service needs to be one of your critical success variables. Alone, quantitative measures of service delivery do not guarantee high quality. For example, simply seeing a child that is reportedly abused or neglected will not ensure that the child is protected. The worker must be thorough, perceptive, and fully informed about child development if the investigation is to be of high quality.

Because it is largely a matter of subjective judgment, quality control is difficult to manage. It generally cannot be reduced to numbers on charts. It must be done by professionals who understand the problems of both the clients and the workers, often by a specialized group located in one central office. Even though such a group has the professional expertise to review cases and judge adherence to standards, their work is often resented by those in the field, who consider such a group too far removed from casework. Consequently, recommendations are resisted or ignored. The most effective quality control I have seen has been exercised by teams of workers and supervisors who, on a rotating basis, review a sample of cases. Thus each worker gets to spend some time on quality control review, discussion across work units is enhanced, and workers feel less threatened.

Peer quality review is simply a good idea. For example, peer review in the child abuse investigation program would be relatively simple to implement. One worker from each investigation unit could be asked to serve part time, for perhaps three months, on a team that would review investigation records (I recommend random and anonymous case selection) and report on their perception of the quality of investigation, assessing thoroughness, particularly as to consistency with agency standards, and evaluating the extent to which obvious community contacts were called as part of the investigations. They could be charged to recommend changes in policy and practice that would enhance the quality of investigation. Their recommendations could then be made available to all workers and supervisors. Keeping a central file of their evaluations, with workers and units identified, would enable management to track the quality of the units' work.

Monitoring Special Program Goals. In addition to measures of critical success variables and efficiency, there may be other measures of activity or service delivery that a leader must watch in order to be accountable to various funding sources, political allies or opponents, and elected officials, who may have particular priorities they insist be followed. The agency itself may have interim program goals that should be watched carefully, for example, agencywide goals on affirmative action. Such goals can be monitored in much the same way that critical success variables are monitored, but they should be reviewed periodically, for they have an unusual staying power in the monitoring system. They need to be dropped from reports once their relevance has passed. Otherwise, they inhibit the leader's ability to focus staff on the outcomes that should drive the agency.

Using Monitoring Reports. Essentially, then, regular monitoring tracks critical success variables, funding flow, and important program or political priorities. The methodology for such tracking need not be sophisticated. In a small agency it does not even have to be automated. However, it is essential that the method be used. It must be taken seriously, and it must also be kept in perspective. Take the case of the sanitation department in a major city that once adopted a weight standard for garbage collection. Analysts figured the total tonnage of garbage to be collected each day, and then divided the total by the number of trucks in the fleet. Each was to pick up a certain quota. However, much of the garbage remained uncollected, for sanitation workers would go to the local fire station to hose the garbage down and bring it up to quota weight. In this case, management had set efficiency standards that were far removed from the desired outcome. And since the outcome was not being monitored, workers found the quickest way to satisfy the standard that *was* being monitored. Workers have an uncanny knack for figuring out which data leaders pay attention to. If the data are unrelated to outcomes, or if leaders simply do not show that they are interested in the outcome-relevant data, then the data, just like the garbage, might as well not be collected.

Evaluation

Program evaluation is an absolute necessity. It tells leaders whether or not agency strategy is working. It is also the way to validate the selection of critical success variables, by providing the evidence needed to refine our assumptions about the links between critical success variables and desired outcomes. In addition, it is important for preserving and enhancing funding for human services in a fiscally conservative environment.

Program evaluation is the process of determining whether or not a program or service has delivered its intended outcomes. It involves measuring changes in the welfare of client and community and determining the extent to which those changes can be attributed to the program or service under study. Both of the tricky tasks can be successfully handled to feed directly into agency planning and advocacy.

Let us take an example. Several years ago, I directed a program for senior state executives in North Carolina. The program was a new venture for the state, which had had no prior tradition of executive development. We scheduled a formal evaluation at the end of the second year, when an appeal was to be made to replace the initial federal backing with state funding.

Two of the outcomes identified for this program were that graduates would become better managers of people and of funds. For the first outcome we examined organizational morale, as measured by surveys and confidential interviews with individual employees. The second outcome was assessed via documented examples of cost saving and productivity improvement. The study was conducted by an independent consultant who had not been part of the program design or management.

Although our measures were not perfect, they were the best we could command with the money and time available. The surveys and documented case studies painted a positive picture of program impact. When the program came up for legislative review, the evaluation proved a lifesaver. We got all the questions you would expect: Why did it cost so much? Why was it residential when it would have been cheaper for the university to come to the state capital? Why did the state have to train executives anyway—were they not qualified when they were hired? Armed with the evaluation, our allies in the legislature had solid evidence of management improvement that justified our efforts.

In the end, the legislature backed the program. Certainly, the political strength of the governor and the determination of his secretary of administration had much to do with the legislature's decision. Still, the evaluation study was important, for it gave our natural allies the firm documentation they needed to argue on our behalf. In addition, and perhaps most important, the evaluation yielded a wealth of information about how to enhance executive talent at the state level. We continued to use that information to guide program development even after we had run out of state funds.

Measuring Outcomes

The simple evaluation in the executive program was useful because it documented that the program had delivered its intended outcomes, and that is the principal purpose of an evaluation. Second, it showed that the program was worth what the state paid (the value of productivity improvements exceeded the cost of the program). Finally, it said nothing about whether our effort was efficient or not, although under different circumstances it might have. All three areas warrant discussion.

Leaders have an enduring obligation to show the public that their programs work, that they deliver what they promise. That is the initial task of program evaluation, and there are two parts to the proof. The first is documenting the benefits to clients. The second is showing that the outcomes are the result of the program or service.

Of these two tasks, identifying and measuring outcomes is the easier, for while tricky, it is eminently possible. Difficulties arise over the selection of measures and over tracking clients. There are few perfect outcome measures; most evaluations seek the best available. The executive program evaluation could perhaps have used some instrument that assessed managerial prowess, but there was stiff resistance to this among our clients, and documented examples and interviews seemed to fit the situation better. Had we had more time and a larger budget, we might have pressed for more formal measures. For what we were trying to do, the measures we employed were acceptable.

The more time there is for outcomes to develop, the harder it is to track clients. Even during the two years of the executive program, several of our executives left state government. Compare that to the experience of Head Start, in which thousands of children enroll and for which some outcome measures cannot be tallied until high school careers are complete. Tracking the entire population of Head Start participants through high school would be expensive, if not impossible. A more reasonable approach is to track a representative sample.

Most of the time, the choice of measures will be easy once the outcomes are identified. For example, in the adolescent pregnancy program, the desired outcome of no second pregnancy suggests that we measure number of pregnancies. Since we have specified a two-year frame for that outcome, we should easily be able to track the full population. The child health outcome suggests that we need acceptable measures of child health, such as the incidence of various diseases, and measures of normal development. Much of the confusion about what to measure in evaluation is probably confusion about desired outcomes, which should have been resolved when the program was conceived.

Once outcome measures for either a full population or a sample have been collected, the tricky business of comparison begins. We usually assume that all of the outcomes we measure can be attributed to our program. Is that necessarily true? As Hatry,

Winnie, and Fisk (1981) and others point out, there are a number of ways to find out.

The executive program used the easiest, and the weakest, way to isolate the effect of the program: a before-and-after comparison. By monitoring improvement in managerial performance, employees were documenting how things were different after the program. Whether such an approach is valid depends on whether another factor could account for the change, in this case whether the executives might have improved on their own or by virtue of a general improvement in management. The before-and-after approach was probably satisfactory because the amount of time between the program's initiation and its outcome was relatively short and the likelihood of some sudden general trend toward management improvement was low.

However, my evaluation was subject to the criticism that the improvements occurred simply because the executives were being watched. This so-called Hawthorne effect is always a problem when an evaluation is done without a control group, a group that does not receive a service or activity, against which the group that receives a service can be compared. In this example, we might at least have interviewed employees of managers who had not been in the program to see how many managers had improved in the eyes of their employees.

In human service cases in which the expected benefits are more controversial, and in which clients may be changing rapidly (children, for example), the before-and-after approach is unsatisfactory. The client group needs to be compared with a formal control group that is like the clients in every respect except that they have not received service.

The most formal comparative approach is the controlled experiment, in which participants are randomly assigned either to the experimental group, which receives the treatment or service in question, or to the control group, which does not. One famous controlled experiment involved the Salk polio vaccine: half of the participants received the Salk vaccine, the other half received a harmless solution (not even the technicians who administered the vaccines knew which participant got which vaccine); the results confirmed the effectiveness of the vaccine, and the rest is history.

In an income tax experiment, one-half of a randomly selected group of New Jersey families received a negative income tax in lieu of traditional public assistance; the other families remained on public assistance. Researchers theorized that families would work harder under a negative income tax because of the higher incentive to earn. In fact, those families reduced their hours of work, choosing to trade second incomes for more family time. In a similar experiment, families who received housing vouchers did not move out of their neighborhoods to higher-quality housing and thereby indicated a preference for community and friends over quality of construction.

Still another experiment of interest is one carried out in Mexico to determine whether "Sesame Street" should be translated into Spanish for Mexican television. The control group saw the original English-language version; the experimental group watched "Sesame Street" in Spanish. The experimental group demonstrated significantly greater learning, and the decision was made to provide a Spanish-language "Sesame Street."

The design of experiments inevitably presents the leader with difficult ethical choices. Can any group legitimately be denied service? If so, which groups and under what circumstances? How much information about the experiment should be given to clients and to the public? Given that experiments are expensive and difficult to conduct, it can be very difficult politically to justify depriving one group of service. It seems possible only when the deprivation is relatively short-term, when the impact of the service is truly unclear or the hypothesis to be tested is genuinely moot, and also relatively straightforward. Unfortunately, those conditions seldom hold in human services. Outcomes may be a long time coming, and most human services deal with issues at least as complex as the housing voucher and income tax examples.

When for ethical reasons services cannot be denied (with abused children, for example), the so-called quasiexperimental approach may prove valuable. In this approach, the control group is manufactured from existing data. One type of quasiexperimental design uses time-series data to project what the experimental population would have been like in the absence of the program or service. Studies of crime sometimes use this approach, and they point up its basic weakness. It is very difficult to make projections about poorly understood phenomena. For example, data from the 1970s indicated a steady increase in crime in many urban areas. Most observers believed this to be a long-term trend, probably the result of the breakdown of family and neighborhood as social institutions. As a result, policy response to the problem focused on strengthening law enforcement and building prisons. Data from the 1980s show that the incidence of certain crimes may be declining in some areas, drug-related crimes being a notable exception. Some observers now wonder whether or not the crime boom in the 1970s was a function of the maturing of the baby boom. Perhaps drugs are a more important stimulant of criminal activity than previously thought. If so, building prisons might not have been the appropriate policy action. A simple time-series approach to crime may not help us find out, for it does not deal with the more difficult questions of cause and effect, suggesting that when analysts are dealing with a phenomenon as complex as crime, the time-series approach is to be handled with care.

A safer kind of quasiexperimental design constructs a control group from data on a general population group that is like the experimental group in every way except the experimental service or treatment. Schools do this when comparing experimental classes to standard classes. In social services, programs new to one geographic region can be compared with similar programs in other, similar regions. For example, for the adolescent pregnancy program we could compare the pregnancy rates of our population with rates in neighboring counties, or with the rates of young women who cannot participate in our program. And we could compare the health status of their children to national averages or to data from areas of the country that are like ours in important ways. While such quasiexperiments do not eliminate the risk of error, they do provide a reasonable basis for helping the leader decide whether the program did what it was supposed to do.

When to Evaluate

When should a program or service be evaluated? One answer is obvious—when it is mandated to do so. In the executive program, the evaluation was part of our legislative mandate. And, of course, we also faced a serious threat to our funding. Public life is such that evaluations can and will be made under such circumstances.

Ideally, evaluation is a normal part of the leadership routine and should be carried out when there are sufficient outcome data for making decisions. For the adolescent pregnancy program, for example, data on second pregnancies can easily be collected on a regular basis, though the first month or so must be considered as different, since this is the program's start-up period. Before the data are used for decision making, the program needs a reasonable chance to get working. Formal evaluation should wait until the start-up period is past.

On the other hand, some outcomes cannot be measured for many years. For example, with finishing high school as a desired outcome for children in Head Start, we must wait at least twelve years to measure results. In this case, the leader needs some intermediate outcomes—such as finishing elementary school—but must recognize that the full evaluation will take a long time. An evaluation after the first year will yield little useful information. In short, the evalution should be scheduled when the outcome or outcomes can be measured.

Was the Program Worth It? A Comment on Cost/Benefit Analysis

Documenting that a program does what it is supposed to do is the primary purpose of evaluation. But the question of whether the program is worth what was spent is not far behind it in importance. In the executive program, we were lucky, for it generated a savings five times greater than the cost of the program. While this finding certainly did not go unnoticed, we—wisely—did not structure our entire evaluation around it.

I advise leaders in human services not to spend a lot of time on cost/benefit analyses. This is not because they are difficult to do (there are fine texts that explain how) but because so few people pay attention to them. Even the most sophisticated budget office and legislative fiscal staff members do not worry much about them, probably because the elected officials they work for do not put much stock in them.

The limits on the use of cost/benefit analysis derive from the nature of the analysis and the highly subjective judgment that must be made in expressing outcome benefits in financial terms (benefits are worth different amounts to different people). In the absence of any political consensus as to the worth of life and liberty, a human services cost/benefit analysis based on any particular value or set of values will be highly variable, and will confound even further an already complicated political process. The problem is only aggravated by the fact that the benefits in most human services can be so long in coming. And then when they come, the stream of benefits over time must be discounted to present dollar value. A Head Start child graduating high school eighteen years from now is not necessarily worth less than this year's graduate. Do not ask me to make the tradeoff. The point is that cost/benefit analysis, despite its growing sophistication, is still not very relevant to making hard political choices. The leader will do well just to make a case that a set of benefits was, in fact, delivered in return for a certain expenditure of public dollars. Trying to reduce that set of benefits to dollar amounts is simply not worth the effort, at least not yet.

But Is the Program Efficient?

Should a formal assessment of the efficiency of a program or set of services be part of program evaluation? After all, does the public not have a right to know whether the services have been delivered at the lowest possible price? Unfortunately, many evaluations deal almost exclusively with permutations of this question. They discuss process—were clients treated promptly? were they satisfied? were caseloads up to national average?

Such questions really belong not in a program evaluation but in regular monitoring reports. Efficiency ought to be a regular, ongoing concern. By relegating efficiency questions to evaluations, you risk not recognizing and dealing with them until it is too late. If you are dealing with them all along, then you will have all the documentation you need when questions arise.

Program evaluations are special studies. They must be undertaken to determine whether or not long-range outcomes have unfolded as expected. They should indicate why expected outcomes have not materialized, and they should document other, unintended outcomes that have also resulted. That is a tall enough order.

Despite the rich literature on the subject, I have deliberately avoided a technical discussion of evaluation. The danger of becoming enthralled with the beauty of technique is that you may lose sight of the purpose of monitoring and evaluation. Monitoring should give the leader regular information to guide daily and monthly decisions about program design and operation. It should provide insights as to whether programs are moving toward intended goals. The evaluation process supplements that information by providing, at the earliest feasible moment and at regular intervals thereafter, formal documentation of outcomes. That is really all there is to it.

8

❧❧❧

How Effective Leaders Focus Their Agencies' Efforts

You have now been introduced to the concept of results-oriented management and have seen that identifying outcomes and critical success variables can be a powerful new approach to planning, budgeting, monitoring, and evaluation. In this chapter you will learn exactly why critical success variables provide greater focus, and thus greater effectiveness, to a human services agency.

To explain the power of results-oriented management, it is useful to contrast the effectiveness of focused planning and monitoring with another management strategy—one that is more popular but less effective—namely, reorganization. Reorganization is often used to move an agency toward its vision. It has a strong lure for elected officials and career program managers. This chapter begins by taking a close look at reorganization as a strategy for focusing agency effort. On the basis of that assessment, it then returns to results-oriented management as a simpler, more effective tool.

The Lure of Reorganization

A few years ago, I led an informal working group of North Carolina mental health managers charged with generating new ideas for managing the state's mental health system, which, like so many human services systems, was struggling to make sense of a morass of programs spreading across several service areas. Services were being delivered by a combination of state institutions, county agencies, and independent operations. Because it was an era of funding reductions, there was considerable conflict over the role and relative funding levels for institutional versus community services. The managers' first reaction was to propose reorganizing area programs and institutions into regional units, each with separate authority over its own budget and service delivery. Luckily, the proposal was never implemented, for it would certainly have cost much more than would have been saved through the reorganization.

Like so many human services managers and policy makers, these managers found the lure of reorganization very strong. Efficiency studies that propose reorganizing operations seem to inevitably follow the election of a new governor. In the 1970s, umbrella human services agencies were created in many states in an attempt to integrate related services into coherent programs and to provide more control to elected and appointed executives. Even now, the typical solution when service inadequacies are made public is reorganization, often at great cost to the politicians who must get the reorganization plans enacted and to the executives who must devote extra time to changing working relationships as they implement the new structures.

Is reorganization really the best way to help an agency realize its service goals? Should organizational restructuring really be the first step in solving management problems? My answer to both questions is no. Restructuring is difficult for the manager to control. I believe that the potent techniques of results-oriented management will accomplish the same goals much more productively. A clear understanding of outcomes and critical success variables enables a manager to plan, budget, and monitor and evaluate to achieve stunning results without the pain and suffering that accompany reorganization.

Let us once again look at the example of Florida's Health and Rehabilitative Services, which shows the problems that can come with a headlong rush into reorganization and also the power of carefully focused planning and monitoring.

The Case of Florida's Department of Health
and Rehabilitative Services

Prior to 1969, Florida, like many states, delivered human services through a variety of independent agencies. When the 1968 state constitution called for reorganizing related, fragmented services into single agencies, the Florida legislature created the Department of Health and Rehabilitative Services (DHRS) by combining Correction, Family Services, Health, Mental Health, Retardation, Vocational Rehabilitation, and Youth Services. The new department was headed by a secretary appointed by the governor. In 1973, Aging and Children's Medical Services were added. All of the former departments became divisions of the new umbrella agency.

Although the legislature had intended to integrate services, the compromises made during enactment derailed the effort. First, the various divisions retained authority over their field offices, allowing those units to operate independently from other divisions' field offices. Second, the division directors were now to be appointed directly by the governor, not by the secretary, a provision that further solidified divisional independence.

Dissatisfaction with this arrangement arose quickly. By 1973, legislators had proposed further reorganization. Representative Richard Hodes, chair of the Health and Rehabilitative Services Committee and a physician, wanted the various divisions to be consolidated into three larger divisions. Hodes complained that DHRS could not provide "reasonable answers to reasonable questions, such as the number of clients being served, the amount of money spent, and the breakdown of administrative and direct service costs" (Lynn, 1980, p. 87). Both the governor and the department opposed the proposal. The governor apparently resisted losing control over the divisions, and the secretary, a former division director, also valued division independence.

The debate continued for two years. In 1974, the president pro tem of the senate claimed, "There is no doubt that the present organization structure of the department encourages the arbitrary pigeonholing of clients, discourages communication and sharing of resources among divisions and creates costly duplication of effort"

(Lynn, 1980, p. 88). The continuing executive opposition finally weakened when Governor Askew's Efficiency Commission recommended reorganization along the lines proposed by the president pro tem, a plan that called for the creation of eleven service districts, each with its own director. The statewide program divisions would be abolished. In addition, each region would have both a single intake system for all clients and case management services to ensure that clients were not arbitrarily shuttled from one service to another. The department counterproposed a compromise plan consolidating the existing divisions into three larger program divisions and creating a system of area coordinators who would oversee department operations across the state.

Political momentum on the issue favored the legislature's plan, which now included making Corrections a separate department, creating the regional structure, with regional administrators but retaining program offices that were essentially remnants of the previous statewide divisions. The regional administrators were to report to the secretary through an assistant secretary for operations. The program offices were to have responsibility for program planning, monitoring, and evaluation, reporting to the secretary through the assistant secretary for program planning and development.

The department was given a year to implement the reorganization. Due to his opposition to the plan, Secretary O. J. Keller was replaced by Pete Page, who was committed to the integration of services but faced considerable difficulty meeting the goal. Since the plan had stipulated staff reduction in the state office, Page lacked sufficient personnel for effective implementation. The National Academy of Public Administration, brought in by Page in 1977 to study the reorganization effort, agreed, stating, "The Legislature has mandated limits without knowing the number of staff necessary to do the job." (National Academy, 1977, p. 54). And the constituents of Vocational Rehabilitation, who never really accepted reorganization, challenged the plan both in the courts and through the Department of Health, Education, and Welfare, continuing the debate into 1979, when Secretary David Pingree (who succeeded Pete Page) negotiated a compromise.

The Verdict Ten Years Later

At first, legislators were pleased with the effects of reorganization. Barry Kutin, who had succeeded Hodes as chair of the House Health and Rehabilitative Services Committee, said, "It's amazing to see the pulling together that's going on in the communities. For the first time there is contact between [D]HRS and all the other agencies—United Fund, the Red Cross, etc. The District Administrator serves as a focal point in the community" (Lynn, 1980, p. 98). Others were skeptical, fearing that authority would remain centralized and that the old guard would not comply with the intent of reorganization. Over time, those fears appeared justified, as advocates and service providers began to complain that no one in the district offices was accountable, that decisions were always referred to Tallahassee, that clients were still being arbitrarily shuttled from service to service, and that there was no effective integration, let alone case management.

These complaints reached a peak in 1985, when a series of grand jury investigations into child welfare deaths vindicated the critics, finding a lack of case management, no integration, and poor casework. Frustrated, the Legislative Oversight Committee invited a second team to evaluate the integration of services achieved through the reorganization. Shortly thereafter, Corey Greer died (see Chapter One).

The National Academy study found that "there are still cracks in the service delivery system, and many individuals fall into them" (National Academy, 1986, p. 20). It offered the example of the intermittently schizophrenic youth who gets bounced back and forth between mental health and developmental services. Particularly in the area of child welfare, policy and procedure argue against integration of services. For instance, abuse and neglect investigation procedures carefully specify that workers are to investigate specific charges, not the family's need for social services.

The authority of the district administrator, the individual charged with leading the integration of services and focusing the department's work on the community, had been limited for the entire decade. The National Academy concluded that district administrators are only as good as the state office allows them to be, since centralized control procedures in budget and personnel effectively keep decision-making authority in the state office. The system is not a decentralized system, it is a centralized system with district administrators.

All of this is not to say that the structure of DHRS is totally inappropriate or that it has had no effect on service delivery in Florida. The state's geographic size and diversity of population certainly argue for some type of regional administration. As the National Academy study observed, there have been some improvements in the transferring of ideas from program to program and district to district.

But the reorganization effort did fail to achieve two of its primary objectives: integration of services and effective regional authority. There are four major reasons for this failure. First, the task of integrating services is very difficult. Because clients often enter the system involuntarily, they sometimes resist receiving any service at all. Parents accused of child abuse may resent the department's very presence in their lives. Clients of Cuban descent find the prospect of state intervention in family matters unacceptable.

Even when clients seek or accept service, their problems, as mentioned earlier, are often so numerous and complex that to understand and respond to any single problem is difficult. The Greer case, as we have seen, began with a medical problem, but the parents had income and child care worries, and there was intrafamilial strain, too. In such a situation, the human services agency's ability to intervene effectively is impeded by lack of knowledge; the difficulties of analyzing the case are compounded by the uncertain links between social and psychological factors.

The second reason for the apparent ineffectiveness of Florida's reorganization is the collision between the rising demands for services and the static resources. Between 1975 and 1985, the state's population increased by 10 percent; social services caseloads increased at an even faster rate. Child abuse reports, for example, increased by 132 percent. On the surface, the legislature appears to have been quite generous: the department's overall budget increased from $886 million to $2.7 billion; the average AFDC payment nearly doubled. However, when adjusted for inflation and the growth in caseloads, real expenditure per client barely held its own. In some areas, such as child welfare, it declined. The problem was built into the reorganization plan, for in an effort to save money, funds were cut, by as much as 50 percent in some cases.

The third, and perhaps most serious, reason for Florida's failure is the enduring split between the operations staff and the program (policy development) offices. The operations staff never had effective authority, which remained with the program offices (the former division offices), whose staff included experts in areas (such as health) where technical expertise and education are important credentials for authority. The district administrators, who were generalists, lacked confidence to assert their authority while the experts were watching in the wings. Secretary Keller had foreseen this problem, recognizing that administrative roles and responsibilities were becoming very unclear. He complained, "I'm the Secretary and I'm sitting in Tallahassee. Up to this time I've been able to say to my Division Directors, 'You're the mental health expert, what's happening?' . . . Now, I'll call a District Administrator and tell him that he's not following the plan [drawn up in Tallahassee], and he'll say, 'Those crazy people in Tallahassee will put anything on paper. They don't have to run the program.' Look at how many programs you have given me to handle down here— nine. Why pick on me just because they have a problem at the mental hospital? Look at the good job I'm doing for you in Drug Rehab" (Lynn, 1980, p. 94).

Like the limits on funding, this ambiguity in roles was rooted in the early debates on reorganization. The ambiguity about the future of the division offices made compromise easier.

By 1985, confusion had eroded into antagonism. In the case of Corey Greer, the workers simply failed to implement the state's policy of prohibiting overcrowding at foster homes. One supervisor claimed to be unaware of the policy. Many similar regulations were instituted after a child's death or other disaster, without full discussion and involvement of the operations staff who would be charged with implementing them. District administrators, who had a very limited role in making policy, increasingly seemed to defer decisions to program specialists, who were frustrated because they had no formal authority to implement their recommendations. The National Academy found that in such an environment, integration across service areas "taxes creativity and results in prolonged decision making, a high degree of bureaucratization, duplication of functional services across units and underutilization of personnel" (National Academy, 1986, p. 6).

In the midst of this confusion, no decision-support systems were ever put into place. The Department, with 28,748 employees in eleven districts when first created, lacked a clear mechanism for setting goals and communicating them throughout the districts. The client information system still does not make information on service delivery available on a timely basis. The budget process gives more voice in setting priorities to the program offices than to the district administrators, who are supposed to act as a voice for their districts in service planning.

These factors—the difficulty of the task, the increasing demands facing the department, the ambiguous distinction between program and operations roles, and the lack of decision-support systems—explain in large part why reorganization did not lead to integration of services. Field workers and their supervisors did not coordinate their efforts on behalf of the individual client. They were not held accountable for specified improvements in the client's life. And management was unable to respond when insurmountable difficulties were encountered. Reorganization led workers away from integration rather than toward it. Program goals became confused when the program/operations split clouded policy development. Reorganization detoured around accountability because managers were too busy fighting political battles and trying to balance caseload and budget realities.

The Importance of Process and Systems

Florida really is no further along the road to integration of services than it was a decade ago. The state is only now grappling with how to initiate case management and outcome-driven control systems at the state and district levels. The Florida experience teaches four lessons about the use of structural reorganization.

First, managing government operations through organizational restructuring is extremely difficult, as Lynn (1980) shows for human services, not only in Florida, but in other states as well.

Changing organizational structures usually requires a strong political constituency to overcome inertia and opposition to change. Building the needed coalition often complicates the political agenda in ways that program the organizational change to failure, as when efficiency advocates in Florida succeeded in reducing the staff available to Secretary Page to implement reorganization, all the while setting an expectation that worked against his efforts at integration. Executive time spent on the political exigencies of organizational change must be borrowed from the time needed to deal with internal issues. The four years that the Florida DHRS head was responding to the complaints of the Vocational Rehabilitation constituency could have been spent sorting out vague program goals and reporting on intradepartmental relationships. It took HRS at least five years to implement the new organizational structure; and there are some who maintain that the implementation is still incomplete.

The second lesson from Florida's experience is that complex problems do not necessarily require complex organizational structures. In fact, just the opposite may be true. Organization theorists have argued that the more complicated a problem, the more flexible the organizational structure should be. Mintzberg (1979) recommends an *adhocracy* structure for a complex organization, which emphasizes shifting the groupings of professionals as problems change. Weick (1969) holds that managers should be more concerned with building "interlocked behavior cycles" than with organization charts, and must coordinate decision-making *processes,* not groups. March and Olsen (1979) maintain that managers can better affect the outcome of the game by "tilting the playing field" rather than trying to direct the action, meaning concentrate on the flow of information and the organizational culture rather than on reporting relationships. Peters (1978) believes the way to influence change is to manage symbols and "daily message-sending activities," such as office routine, priorities, and the leader's calendar.

This is not so surprising, given that human services workers typically handle large caseloads with limited resources and are expected to assume full responsibility for an adverse client outcome. If agency goals are unclear and the measures of accountability vague, then many of the behaviors observed in Florida become comprehensible, even though undesirable: workers delay decisions as long as possible; complex cases are not referred so as not to create more work; workers and supervisors avoid communicating with one another, in the hopes that ignorance will excuse breaking unrealistic agency regulations. Rhetoric that does not match performance capabilities is quickly drained of meaning, and morale suffers.

It is encouraging to see how many workers in Florida continue their dedication to compassionate casework, even without clear guidance on goals. Their work might be made easier if the structure were simpler, but it would help enormously if the goals were clearer, the measures of accountability dependable, and the process for case management straightforward.

These observations raise the fourth lesson: changing organizational structure should be the *last* strategy a manager uses in directing line operations. First the manager should try to clarify the decision-making process in service delivery, create an information system that allows for outcome-derived measures of accountability, and allow, indeed force, broad participation in policy planning and development. The manager should also develop a training program that orients staff toward desired outcomes and focuses their energies on critical success variables. Then individuals, and agency units, will begin to generate their own ideas for organizational restructuring that respond to the requirements of the agency's mission. When restructuring is tried first, in the absence of clarity on goals and accountability, the manager is inviting powerful figures from outside the agency to specify the managerial agenda. As in Florida, doing so will surely distract the agency from its appointed responsibilities. In all likelihood, Florida's DHRS could successfully deliver services from a variety of organizational structures. If there is a one best structure for that agency, no one has found it and no one can guarantee that it will be best in the future.

Enter Results-Oriented Management

Against the backdrop of the Florida experience, we can profitably return to the six steps of results-oriented management. The Florida case shows that managers have considerably more authority over program planning and monitoring than they do over organizational structure. The challenge is to use that authority in a way that will move the agency toward its vision. The manager must be able to focus diffuse energy within the agency on client problems. As the Florida case shows, you cannot do that unless you have a clear sense of what outcomes you want to produce and for which clients. Having a focused vision means you are prepared to translate that vision into performance standards and monitoring processes that will lead your agency toward client-centered outcomes. Armed with critical success variables, you can exploit the latent strength of planning, budgeting, and monitoring systems while avoiding the obvious trap of overloading those systems. With an understanding of critical success variables, you can translate desired outcomes into clear performance expectations for individuals and work units. You can put outcomes and critical success variables to work in monitoring and evaluation. Quite simply, you can give even the most complex human services agency a client-centered discipline.

One social services agency that I know is experimenting with a client-driven structure. Service workers are grouped in teams that deal with different age groups. Services for mothers and infants are based in a local health clinic; the team includes income maintenance and protective services workers in addition to public health nurses. Services for children are based in schools. Services for the elderly are clustered around day programs. The various groups of team professionals gather periodically to compare notes.

A similar structure would make great sense in Florida, where each district could be organized in age-group teams. Creating them would involve consolidating the current district-based program and operating staffs into a single set of service delivery teams. It might well reduce the operating staff's current dependence on state program offices. It would certainly be easier to deal with than the current structure.

This is not the only way to structure human services. However, with clearly articulated outcomes and critical success variables, such organizational schemes are easily implemented. Once outcomes and critical success variables are used to structure management systems, people can group themselves in ways that focus most effectively on the client. Structure will then become a way to position resources to be of most use to clients. The integration of work effort, rather than being the result of complex reporting arrangements, will be the product of management systems that discipline the agency to respond to clients. The evolution of the structure can be incremental and flexible. Structure will always be in process. It will always be simple, and people will be productive.

9

Keeping Programs Responsive
to New Demands

"What got you there won't keep you there," a good friend of mine always says when he begins a management development course. The skills, knowledge, and environmental factors that contribute to building a program will not necessarily sustain that program in the face of changing demographics, politics, or community expectations. Residential programs for children, popular not so many years ago, are in declining use. Our populations of elderly citizens are growing to the point that in many areas they already strain our service delivery capacity. The aging of the baby boom presents a large middle-aged population to community mental health centers. What's a leader to do?

So far, we have concentrated on current and near-term leadership challenges. Having a clear focus on the present is not enough, however. Programs and agencies must change as the communities around them change and as the social problems they deal with change. Strategic thinking is a way of articulating a vision that will help keep that vision relevant, and is key to long-term leadership success. This chapter presents a framework for strategic thinking in human services.

What Is Strategy?

The concept of *strategy* is well accepted in the corporate world. Andrews (1971) looks at it as a statement of goals and policies that define what business a corporation is in and what kind of organization it will be. Ansoff (1965) speaks of strategic decisions—those that deal with the business firm's relationship with the environment, for example, product and market decisions. Ansoff (1979) believes that an organization has achieved success when its product and market decisions match the environment. Steiner (1969) considers a company's strategy as the statement of where it wants to go, and Steiner (1979) suggests that company strategy must be a statement that sets parameters for subsequent decisions about production, marketing, finance, and personnel. Tregoe and Zimmerman (1980) define strategy as the statement of what an organization wants to become and how it will get there—in their words, "the framework which guides those choices that determine the nature and direction of an organization" (p. 17).

Strategy can be distinguished from tactics, which refers to the day-to-day deployment of specific resources to achieve short-run goals. We are using tactics when we deploy troops on a particular battlefield, or when we oversee a unit of child welfare workers for a month of child abuse investigation. Strategy deals with the longer term. It is the plan for the deployment of all resources to meet overall agency goals. As strategy in war is the plan that shows how the coordinated movements of various troop units will lead to victory, so in human services strategy discusses how various agency units will, by working together, achieve a desired effect on the community over time. Strategy sets the framework for tactics. It defines what the agency will do and what kind of organization the agency aspires to be. Most simply, strategy is the overall statement of what services the agency provides, to what clients, and for what purposes. Just as a battle plan must be updated after a reassessment of victories and defeats, so must an agency's strategy be revised periodically to keep up with changes in the community.

Strategy, then, is a mapping of agency capabilities onto the needs of the community. It is a concise statement of what the agency can and will do about the problems and needs related to its basic mission. For example, one apparent strategy of the Lutheran Family Services agency discussed in Chapter Two was to provide high-quality group-home services for emotionally disturbed youth in order to facilitate their adjustment to community life, either with their natural families or in alternative community settings. That strategy, though it captures most of what the agency is doing, has never actually been articulated. As a result, its recent application to get licensed as an adoption agency was turned down because, lacking an explicit strategy, the agency did not recognize that its strengths at serving troubled youth did not necessarily equip it to work in adoption.

Lutheran Family Services was right to broaden its service base, for it had only one client group—Willie M. children—and one principal source of funding. What if the state decided to cut its funding? The environment that had led to the rapid growth of Willie M. funding had changed, and the legislature was increasingly suspicious of programs funded through class action suits rather than normal appropriation channels. Lutheran Family Services needed to review its strategy to ensure its long-term relevance to a changing community.

Clearly, what Lutheran Family Services wanted to do was to redirect its existing strengths toward other pressing community needs. To do that, leadership needs to assess those strengths, compare them to its vision of a changing community, and consider alternatives that might balance the two. It needs the sort of fit that Ansoff suggests for corporations. As Tregoe and Zimmerman (1980) suggest, any organization, public or private, can succeed only if it has a strategy that is relevant to the environment around it and that it can implement successfully. Developing such a strategy may be new to many human services leaders, but luckily, the writings on corporate strategy can help us. Levin (1981), in particular, engagingly offers a set of simple steps for devising a strategy: the leader sizes up the organization and the environment and evaluates alternatives for matching the two. To follow his advice, Lutheran Family Services would do the following.

1. Assess the organization and its strengths.
2. Assess the opportunities and risks in the environment.
3. Map organization strengths onto the environment.

Assessing the Organization

The starting point for strategic thinking is the present. Development for the future is based on the resources, expertise, and strengths that you have now. To avoid making a strategic error, such as Lutheran Family Services' premature entry into infant adoption, you need to assess your current position honestly and accurately. First you need to look at your history, for as Winston Churchill once said, you can only see as far into the future as you can into the past. Knowing your history will help you assess agency strengths and weaknesses. Then you will be better able to map your strengths onto the environment. The following paragraphs explain why understanding your agency's history and strengths and weaknesses is important to strategic thinking.

Looking at Agency History

Momentum. Organizations learn and change over time, and the sum total of that learning can be a resource for the strategizing leader. Organizations have a momentum that derives from their history. At any point in time, they are moving in a certain direction, and at a particular pace. To build strategy, the manager needs to know both pace and direction. For example, since its founding in the late 1970s, Lutheran Family Services has grown to a staff of 200 and a budget of $5 million. The pace has been hurried, and the direction clearly toward being a Willie M. agency. Since clients, community groups, and the state are now skeptical of its ability to handle other services, the agency is in trouble unless leadership can control pace and direction. The pace must be slowed, or the agency puts its reputation for quality services on the line. The direction toward exclusive service to Willie M. children must be altered lest agency options be severely restricted.

Tangible Assets. Over the course of their history, organizations also derive financial equity. Prudently managed agencies, especially voluntary ones, will increase their endowments and stock of tangible assets over time. Government organizations can do the same, either directly through special funds for clients, or indirectly in physical plant and technology. These sources of equity are very important, for they set limits on what the agency can do in the future.

Staff Skills and Knowledge. Even more important than tangible assets are the intangible sources of equity, which the leader must also assess. Perhaps the most significant of these are the skills and knowledge of staff. When clients and service technology change rapidly, the ability of staff to generate innovative solutions to unprecedented problems is an extraordinary asset. A wise leader will assess and then draw upon the unique skills and knowledge base of his agency in planning strategy.

Agency Reputation. Agencies also build a reputation with key constituents, becoming known and respected for their ability to help solve problems important to clients, politicians, and community groups. The strength and extent of that reputation can be leveraged into new opportunities if recognized and put to work. Lutheran Family Services might have been spared its adoption fiasco if it had first consulted those who knew and respected its work.

Political and Service Alliances. Alliances built over time are important resources when planning agency strategy. This includes collaborative protocols with other agencies that build the trust that enables others to go to bat for you politically. A wise leader will recognize such alliances at the outset of planning, consider how to use them for future advantage, and avoid damaging them. For example, the alliance between LFS and the state Willie M. manager might be hurt now that Social Services has reported negatively on the adoption issue. Strong alliances with community groups might give an agency a strategic advantage in, say, adoptions of children with physical or emotional handicaps: community groups (such as churches) can provide valuable assistance in finding appropriate homes for such children. Only by recognizing the strength of the alliance can strategy possibly be developed.

Agency Tradition. Tradition can be a troublesome thing, but as Churchill understood, leaders can use tradition to their advantage. Many a manager has been confronted with resistance to change: "We have never done that here," or "We did that ten years ago and it didn't work." That is tradition at its worst. Tradition at its best keeps people focused on and enthusiastic about their basic mission. A century and a half ago, a group of devoted Methodist deaconesses founded a hospital in Boston to care for those who could not afford it elsewhere. To this day, New England Deaconess Hospital upholds the tradition of those women, called angels of mercy by one Boston newspaper. The hospital still provides compassionate care to those who cannot receive it elsewhere. In an interesting twist of strategy, the hospital now serves those afflicted by serious, difficult-to-treat diseases, such as heart disease and cancer, rather than indigent patients. The tradition has been adapted to a world with public hospitals and government-funded health insurance by focusing on a particular client population that still needs help.

Assessing Agency Strengths and Weaknesses

Once you know your agency's history, you are ready to compile a list of agency strengths and weaknesses. This is the focus of your organizational assessment. There are several aspects of agency life to inventory.

The Program. First, and perhaps most obvious, is the program. Which services are of high quality and which are not? Where are the programs' strengths and where are the limitations? At LFS, the service providing group homes for Willie M. children was strong, whereas some of the refugee resettlement services were strong, others not. All programs were concerned about maintaining quality control throughout a growing service area while the administrative machinery to support a rapidly growing set of service units seemed to be bogging down in paperwork.

Staff. Where does staff have or lack experience? How high is turnover? How good is morale? Is the staff well trained? What are its special competencies? (This last borrows the effective corporate strategy of doing those things that one does better than anyone else.)

Finances. How solid is your funding base? Does it rely on a single stream of funds that may be vulnerable to political change, or is there a healthy diversity of sources? How resilient is the agency in finding new funds to make up for lost monies? Do you decide what programs to offer on the basis of your funding streams, or do you look for funds for the programs that will provide highest benefit levels for your clients? What is the status of your nonfinancial physical resources—such as office space and equipment?

Community Standing. Does your governing board provide strong policy guidance? Does it know what is going on in the community and inside the agency? How are you regarded by key political figures—your department head, the governor and the governor's office, budget and fiscal staff, legislative leaders? How much political capital do you have to draw on, and from where? In the case of Lutheran Family Service's attempt to move into adoption, since it was dealing with a state agency—Social Services—with which it had had no prior experience, it lacked any preexisting credibility with that agency. In addition, Willie M. programs are funded through its Mental Health division, which has a history of antagonism toward Social Services. Thus, LFS's move to adoption really played none of its strengths save solid community contact via its link to the network of Lutheran churches.

Assessing the Environment

In Chapter Three, we talked about forecasting the major trends affecting your clients. You will need to recognize those trends in planning strategy. You need to consider what those trends mean for your clients and constituents. For example, the changing demographics of fertility and migration in California suggest that by the end of the century, client population there will represent a very different mix of cultural traditions—significantly more Hispanics, Asians, and blacks. Health officials will face increasing demands for health care from the elderly. In fact, there are likely to be increasing demands across a wide array of programs serving the elderly, from day activities to nutrition to wellness support. Lutheran Family Services would do well to consider the political limits on the number of children who can qualify as Willie M., and

recognize growth in other difficult-to-treat youth groups, such as
the mentally ill and mentally retarded.

The forecasting exercise in Chapter Three should generate
the information you need for your environmental assessment,
except in one important area—your competition. You might not be
accustomed to thinking about competition in human services, since
the possibility that not-for-profit agencies compete is recent. And
yet, competition is growing—for both public and voluntary
agencies. For public agencies, there is competition for dollars.
Human services must compete with education, transportation,
housing, and so on. Leaders in human services must know what
issues, problems, and proposals are in the works in those other areas
if they are to plan realistically for themselves. For voluntary
agencies, there is increasing competition from the profit-making
sector. In Illinois, for example, better than one-third of all state
contracts for home health nursing for the elderly are held by profit-
making organizations. Those agencies enter carefully selected
markets in which they believe they can deliver better service than
existing agencies, and do so at a profit. What they are about and
how they approach various markets is critical for the voluntary
agency leader to know.

Mapping Strengths onto the Environment

The growth of competition in human services only serves to
highlight the wisdom of reassessing strategy to ensure that agency
objectives are consistent with community evolution. The shrewd
leader must evaluate existing services and new ideas for services as
to their long-run impact on the community, provide those services
that have high impact now and in the future, and make sure the
service portfolio is changing to accommodate changes in the
community. In securing a place in a network of competing service
agencies, the leader will want to understand the agency's distinctive
competencies and build a strong service portfolio around it.

This recommendation pertains not only to voluntary-agency
leaders, who often have a great deal of choice over program strategy,
but also to public-agency leaders. Even though government
agencies may have a legislative mandate that specifies agency focus,

leaders must nonetheless keep programs relevant within those limits, by influencing program direction and controlling the flow of funds into those programs. They must ensure that programs evolve as clients change, and play a major role in developing proposals for new services and for changing existing mandates. Government leaders require a coherent strategy to give these otherwise diverse activities a common purpose.

To achieve that coherent strategy demands a way to balance our assessments of agency abilities and environmental needs and trends. Our strategy should be to run programs that have high benefit to the community now and develop programs for the future that respond to the changes we foresee. Some of those programs will rely on our current strengths; those we can develop promptly. Others will test areas of weakness; with them we must proceed cautiously.

The *portfolio approach* to strategy (Henderson, 1970) is common in the private sector. That approach, which charts market share against industry growth, has been justifiably criticized for its dependence on financial return as a criterion for success. However, if we shift the emphasis of the portfolio away from financial measures and toward community impact and a future orientation, it can help us see alternatives for human services.

To help focus your strategic thinking, Figure 1 shows a strategic planning matrix. Here is how it works. Your organizational assessment forms one axis (Expertise), and your environmental assessment forms the other (Program Impact). You list the areas in which the agency has high expertise and those in which it has low expertise. You also list agency activities that are important to the community now and that will have high impact in the future. This two-by-two matrix generates four categories, which help classify the programs or services the agency is currently providing or considering. By classifying the programs, the leader is assessing strategy for the future. Let us go clockwise through the four categories, beginning with the lower left quadrant, Cash Cows.

Building on Your Cash Cows

Agency services with a high current impact and of recognized high quality, and in which the agency has high expertise, are what

Figure 1. Strategic Planning Matrix.

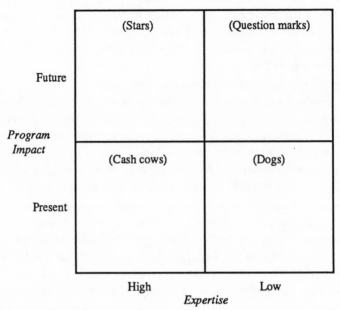

profit makers would consider *cash cows;* that is, they have a high market share and, being relatively efficient to produce, generate cash. Most likely, the agency has lots of experience providing the service, the staff is knowledgeable, and there is a relatively large client population and a proven track record, all of which makes the program highly regarded by clients as well as the constituency that supports it. Such cash cows could be considered the program base for the agency, being what brings recognition, public credibility, and funding.

In human services, we must be careful how we analyze our cash cows. After all, some of our programs may not bring in much cash but rather, public acceptance that is essential to public funding. That is why we must consider community impact, not just funding impact, in assessing the program base, which here is made up of all programs with high current impact on the community, regardless of their financial return.

The base in a program serving the elderly, for instance,

might be a Meals on Wheels service with an established clientele and a proven track record. If the program has been running for any length of time, it is probably operating very efficiently. This is a service on which the agency can build its reputation and to which it can point with pride when it makes its case before public bodies and private funding groups. Moreover, the large client population served can act as a referral pool for other services and a source of ideas for new services.

Such program base services are sometimes cash cows. At Lutheran Family Services, for example, group homes for Willie M. clients are cash cows: they have a high impact on the state, are highly regarded, and generate the bulk of the agency's financial base. In the Florida Department of Health and Rehabilitative Services, on the other hand, foster care and investigations of abuse and neglect are the program base, yet neither program is particularly well funded. They have the longest history and the highest public visibility, and typically are the measure by which the community assesses the agency's effectiveness. Hence, when a child dies in foster care, the community is outraged because it sees the death as indicative of larger problems.

It is essential that Florida's child abuse and neglect investigations and foster care achieve very high quality, even with inadequate funding. Quality review is the key, and the agency must carefully document its accomplishments and activities. Indeed, because of its high visibility, it needs a record of accomplishment in order to build its case for greater public support. The program base should produce examples, with statistical support, that demonstrate its impact on the community. By making such data public, the agency can broaden public support. The public agency must be assertive in informing the public of the successes and activity in its program base, on which everything else at the agency rests.

Developing the Stars

Programs in which your agency has high expertise but that are likely to experience rising community impact in the future fit into the upper left quadrant of the matrix: *stars*. In mental health, programs providing day activities and respite for families of the elderly mentally ill are examples. Day-care services in Florida are another example. Agencies have experience providing both services, and with a high quality. The demand for the services, and their impact on the elderly, children, and families will grow over time. Unlike the basic programs, which have already reached their maximum impact, stars have yet to reach their potential, and so must respond to growing demand with increasing availability and quality.

In human services, stars must be the subject of careful planning and the focus of strong efforts to gain new resources that will make them available as demand for them grows. For instance, in the case of mental health for the elderly, we estimate future demand by adding to the current caseload our estimate of the client consequences of Alzheimer's disease and other such disabilities. The leader must publicize the dimensions of the problem and thereby build a constituency for the service. Decisions makers have to "buy" the problem before you can sell them the solution. The impact of current services should be documented, and then demonstrated persistently to build the case for program expansion.

In the case of day care in Florida, there is little question that the service will be needed more five years from now than at present. Just as a company does market research on demand for a particular product, the Department of Health and Rehabilitative Services needs to gauge how the demand for day care will grow: Who are the various families that will need care? How might their needs be different from today? How will they be distributed geographically? How will they look in terms of income and family structure? What impact will those factors have on the way the care is provided? Star programs require careful planning, beginning with a precise definition of service populations and their needs. Services should be planned in response to those needs, and the data generated in planning should contribute to the building of public support. At Lutheran Family Services, the star program is group homes for adolescents other than Willie M. children. They should be thinking about how that adolescent population will grow and how the already excellent group homes can be adapted to serve that population.

The Need for a Competitive Edge

Leaders must sharpen the competitive edge for the program base and for stars, because both categories are likely to encounter tough competition for funds and perhaps for clients. Certainly, the program base will undergo careful scrutiny, largely as a result of its size and prominence. Other agencies will search for a way to get a piece of the action. They will also have their eyes on the same trends you do, and will also be trying to develop their stars so as to attract growing public support.

How do you achieve a competitive edge in such an environment? Following Porter (1980, 1985), I see three ways. First, you can be a cost leader. That is, you can provide a service more cheaply than anyone else—as in Illinois, where the profit-making agencies argue that it is cheaper for them to provide a home health service than for the state to gear up a service of its own.

Second, you can focus your services on a population that no one else can or will serve, as Lutheran Family Services does with Willie M. children. This strategy may be especially important during budget cutbacks, when for survival you might tailor services to a group the public must serve.

Third, you can differentiate your service from others in significant ways, such as a special measure of quality, a more convenient location or time, or the like. The health department that offers services to adolescents in their schools will surely see a broader cross section than if it waited for those young people to find their way to the public health clinic. By differentiating that service, the health department will be in a strong position to argue for support for its adolescent programs, and those programs will be well positioned to respond to community need as it evolves.

More than likely, you will use some combination of these three strategies to build program stability. For example, you might combine differentiation with focus—build a high-quality program that primarily serves a special population. A home health program for the elderly that specialized in services that would otherwise require expensive hospitalization will have a definite advantage in a cost-conscious future. Similarly, a program for the mentally ill that prevents institutional placement of severely disabled clients will have a compelling case for public support. Thus, what the leader must do in a tough competitive environment (whether for funds or clients) is develop programs that are different, so the agency has a distinctive competence that is obvious to clients and funding agencies alike.

Responding to the Question Marks

There are many promising programs with potential high impact for which your agency has limited expertise. These programs or services are the *question marks* in the upper right quadrant of the matrix. You may not have tried these ideas before, or you may have tried them and had a bad experience. If you can develop your expertise in these areas, they can become high-impact programs in the future.

In the corporate world, question marks might include all sorts of convenience products—from microwavable gourmet foods to disposable diapers for the bedridden. Group home services to mentally retarded/mentally ill clients is such a program for Lutheran Family Services. Teen health clinics in public schools is such a possibility for Florida HRS. Respite care for the elderly is an example for programs that have no prior experience with such services.

To develop a question mark idea, leaders must find a way to cultivate expertise without putting the agency at unacceptable risk. Many companies will use carefully selected test markets to try out new products before introducing them nationally, wishing not to stake a reputation on a product or service that will fail. Lutheran Family Services cannot afford to develop a statewide network of group homes only to discover itself unable to serve the clients in them. The state of Florida would be ill advised to propose the immediate development of teen health clinics in every school, particularly given the fear of many groups that such clinics will engage in family planning. If the clinics were to prove unsatisfactory, the HRS would lose valuable credibility.

HRS and LFS need to find ways to test these new program ideas—pilot programs or experiments that help the agency develop expertise without raising dangerous public expectations. In

Florida, HRS got legislative approval to seek a foundation grant to test one teen health clinic in a rural county. LFS could seek a grant from the Division of Mental Health for a pilot group home. In either case, these test cases must be set up so as to maximize what is learned. Staff should be evaluated on and rewarded for how much they learn about such a service as well as whether or not the experiment is a success.

Taking Care of the Dogs

There is a final category of programs in the matrix. Those are the programs that have reached or passed their time of high public impact and that have never developed expertise—the dogs. They have never run very well, and are going to be of less and less interest and use to clients and constituents in the future. The dogs have a high potential for dragging down the agency, for taking far too much staff and management time, and for distracting you from important work. The potential damage from dogs must be contained. If you were a product manufacturer, you would want to remove these dogs from market shelves.

In the public sector, ending services is a difficult and delicate process, however. For Lutheran Family Services, for example, refugee resettlement is, in three of four locations, a dog. Designed to relocate Southeast Asian families, the program has had success only in the one community where it was able to hire a Vietnamese, who was already a leader there. Although many human services agencies would probably spend management time locating Vietnamese staff in the other three communities to replicate the success, in fact the number of refugees assigned to LFS is declining, so it would be better to close the other three programs. Luckily, Lutheran Family Services can probably close the refugee resettlement projects with little difficulty, for they have a short history and few passionate advocates and obstinate defenders. However, in many other cases, where the advocates and defenders are ready to fight, you need substitutes before you can ease the dog out of the program portfolio.

One effective strategy is to "starve" the dog, that is, gradually cut off funds and clients until even program defenders admit the

program should go. A leader who once had to close a training
school used this strategy to perfection. He began by establishing a
policy that all youth would be served in the least restrictive settings,
and as close to their homes as possible. Gradually, as community
alternatives appeared, youth were sent to them rather than to the
school. The leader stopped capital improvement projects at the
school, and within four years the number of clients involved was
small enough to easily get consensus to close the facility. This was
aided, incidentally, by the leader's practice of including cost per
youth served in his monthly management report to the department
head, because over time the report clearly showed cost per youth at
the school was rising above comparable costs in the community.
That evidence was seen regularly by legislative staff, and so even the
legislature began to question the school's operation. (We might call
this "sending the dog into the street to play.")

Under some circumstances, a dog can be adopted successfully
by another agency. A Pennsylvania Children's Aid Society began a
parent support group to help parents of children it served work
through problems together. The effort was so successful that other
parents joined and the group soon embarked on a wide range of
activities, many of little direct benefit to the society. These activities
began to compete with staff and financial needs of other programs.
The agency, as a United Way recipient, could not raise funds for the
support group independently. Thus, the erstwhile success had
become a dog. At the suggestion of the staff, the parent group
incorporated as a separate nonprofit entity, giving it access to funds
that the society could not get for it.

If none of this works, then the dog must be put in a kennel.
Unfortunately, many agencies spend far too much time trying to
turn dogs into cash cows, a risky effort. It is better to restrict the
amount of time, energy, and money devoted to dogs.

The Case for a Portfolio of Services

One of the interesting aspects of a strategic planning matrix
is that it too changes with time. Unfortunately, while the communities we serve are dynamic, many agencies have static strategies.
Strategies must change, and they must change in an uncertain

climate. The program base of today becomes the dog of tomorrow. Some of the programs that are stars now do not develop into strong elements of the program base. Key staff might leave; other agencies may develop a better approach. And you can never be sure how your experiments with question marks will turn out.

Therefore, most agencies should plan strategy by developing a strong portfolio of services that provides several carefully selected stars and question marks in addition to their program base. As time passes, the stars, if carefully envisioned, can develop into part of the program base. Some of the experiments will work, and some current question marks will become stars. The program base, if managed for high quality and accountability, can give you maximum support for new program ventures.

One of the interesting advantages of a portfolio approach to services is the flexibility it gives to fund raising. For example, a highly visible program base is often necessary to secure individual contributions and public funds. Lutheran Family Services, if it can document its success with difficult kids, has a natural audience of Lutherans who would be happy to help. Certainly, the nay sayers among the policy makers will be quieted by evidence that LFS can, in fact, help the youth that no one else can help.

Corporate funders, on the other hand, are often attracted to stars. Corporations fund not-for-profit ventures to gain public attention. They like to get a long-term return for their initial investment. Stars are perfect for them. Because your expertise is proven, there is little risk of adverse publicity. Because the need is growing, the company can get in on the ground level.

Just as corporations do not like risks, foundations embrace them. They value innovative projects at the cutting edge of service delivery. They often do not mind failure so long as something new and exciting is learned. Foundations are ideal funding sources for question marks.

To see how a portfolio can aid strategy, let us consider the case of the fictitious Union County Health Department. The department is fairly traditional in its services, with its primary programs being the provision of blood tests for couples applying for a marriage license and preschool immunizations. Over the past several years, it has given fewer immunizations, as middle- and upper-income children have tended to get theirs from private physicians. The department offers some prenatal care for low-income women but depends on private physicians to screen and treat young children. Because reimbursement rates are low, many children receive no service. The department traditionally has provided very little service to the elderly and currently has no programs for them at all.

Union County has a traditional manufacturing base in textiles and furniture, whose factories survived the recession and which, despite much automated production in textiles, still employs many workers. Both textile and furniture plants use chemicals that have uncertain long-term effects. The county has a large low-income population and a rapidly growing elderly population, many of whom depend on Social Security for their income. Nearly one in three pregnancies is to an unwed mother; over half the unwed mothers are teenagers.

The Union County Health Department has an unhealthy strategy for the future. Its program base and testing and inoculation programs are declining in importance. Unless the director shows that the department is providing high-quality and extensive coverage, especially to low-income children who cannot receive inoculations elsewhere, the department may be in trouble. The department needs to document the impact on clients, the extent of coverage, and the services' effect on public health. The star at present is the perinatal program. The department needs to develop that service, extending it, perhaps through outreach efforts that regularly bring screening clinics to factories, schools, and churches. The director must aggressively pursue options that increase the flow of funds into the program, particularly federal entitlement funds, and should begin to build a case showing how much can be saved by avoiding future disability through effective early screening.

The Union County question marks include a whole range of services to the elderly and occupational screening and health promotion ventures, in which the department has no experience. The director should pursue ways to develop pilot programs in both areas. In services to the elderly, one-day respite programs are desirable, perhaps in coordination with churches or other volunteer groups that already serve the client group. This avoids extending a long-term commitment in an area in which the director cannot be sure competence will develop. In occupational health, a screening and education program in conjunction with a local industry could work. While some industries might resent intrusion, others might welcome help, especially considering the potentially serious health hazards. The director should be ready to grab opportunity, but careful not to promise a service that cannot be delivered.

The County's dogs may well be its inoculation and testing programs. The decision about their status depends on the size of the population currently served, its likely growth, and the quality of service. If population size is declining and the quality is barely acceptable, then the director should find other ways to serve these clients. Services provided on contract by private physicians or school nurses might be an answer. If the population is growing and the quality is low, then the director must begin to improve quality. A part of the program base is in jeopardy.

We now have a rough outline of the Union County strategy: the Health Department provides screening and education services to vulnerable populations, selective treatment services to those who cannot afford private care, and support for families who must care for dependents with health concerns, especially the very young and the elderly. To make this strategy more specific, we need additional information, which we do not have. Still, this case shows how a leader in human services can use the portfolio approach to plan agency strategy.

Planning Strategy: You Can Do It, But Don't Do It Alone

Once you enter your current services and new program ideas into the planning matrix, you are well on your way to articulating a strategy. You have a clear sense of what services you will provide, for which clients, and for what purposes. Planning strategy is fun, and not as difficult as you might imagine. But guard against going too fast. I remember an executive who ran to the telephone during a strategic planning seminar break to tell his assistant to "shoot" a dog. That program, on close analysis, turned out to have a much brighter future than the executive thought. It was, in fact, not a dog but a question mark. Rushing through strategic planning as outlined here carries the risk of confirming old prejudices or generating new ones. You can reduce that risk, and increase the likelihood that your strategy will be implemented successfully, if you don't try to do it all by yourself. Gather your staff together and invite them to think through the organization's history and strengths and weaknesses. Get them in on your organizational assessment. Then let them investigate and discuss the service environment. Let the manager of a dog discover the declining market himself. Lead the manager of a star toward her own discovery of the potential for the program. Then let the staff classify your programs on the strategic planning matrix. What they discover, they will own. Your job will be much easier, and you will learn a lot from them.

Strategy, after all, is vision. If that vision is not shared, the strategy is mere words on paper. You want a strategy that is alive, that guides program decision making every day, and that responds to changes in the service environment. You must lead the strategic thinking, but you need not do it all alone. One of the helpful characteristics of the strategic planning framework presented in this chapter is that you can use it to help your staff focus on strategic opportunities. I have had particular success in retreats that focus on this framework along with the forecasting matrix in Chapter Three. Typically attended by all program managers, the day of retreat is structured around the process of strategic thinking. They begin by listing their organization's historical events, gleaning from them a feeling for program momentum and agency equity. Then they compile lists of strengths and weaknesses. Next, in small groups, they complete the forecasting matrix, and in discussing it develop a shared view of the future. With that done, the staff completes the strategic planning matrix, the discussion of which teaches them all about the broader operation of the agency.

If participants have a second day, they can usefully debate and select a set of program priorities based on the insights gained from the strategic planning matrix. They then ought to pledge to review the priorities regularly (perhaps every six months) and reassess the planning matrix at least annually. If they do, the leader will find that the people in the organization will in fact keep the leader informed of how their shared vision should be kept up to date.

10

❧❧❧❧

Creating Climates
That Encourage Change

Everything in the earlier chapters suggests that leaders must be catalysts for change. They have the responsibility for creating a climate in which individuals and agencies can adapt policies and programs to changing client and constituent demands. There is a continual challenge to build coalitions that can protect programs from unwarranted opposition and build a persuasive case for human services in the face of stiff competition for funds.

Leaders are the agents of change not only in human services but in all enterprises, as has been noted in traditional studies of leadership (Sayles, 1979) and some more recent studies prompted by the need for American industry to reassert competitiveness (Burgelman and Sayles, 1986; Kanter, 1983; Peters and Waterman, 1982). However, the constraints on change agents in human services are numerous and all too often overwhelming. The leader typically does not have authority over the full range of agencies that provide human services to a specific group of clients. Groups of employees and almost all advocacy groups have their own agendas for change, some of them quite limited. Political alliances are constantly shifting, and all political support in human services is vulnerable to the unpredictable crisis (the death of a child, for example).

So how can the leader create a climate in which promising new ideas flourish? in which coalitions for new approaches to programs and clients receive a fair trial? in which programs have a chance to adapt to clients? It is unfortunate that many human services managers probably believe that climates for change are simply impossible for most managers to create or sustain. Too few human services agencies have a tradition of advocacy for change. Most are responsive to initiatives from the outside without themselves being assertive proponents of new ideas. As a result, there is a meager body of case studies on the subject. Fortunately, there are a few good examples, including a recent one in which the Maine Department of Human Services played a major role in creating a climate to support significant changes in that state's legal proceedings in child abuse cases. This chapter examines the Maine experience and draws from it a few lessons about how human services leaders can build policy environments receptive to new ideas.

The Garrianna Quinn Case

Garrianna Quinn was first referred to the Maine Department of Human Services in May 1982. The case record of the physician who examined her for serious bruises at a rural hospital showed: "The entire left side of her face was bruised from the hairline to jaw and back to her left ear. The left eye was the color of a purple plum and swollen completely shut. Her right eye was similarly colored and swollen, but open enough to allow her to see" (State of Maine, 1984a, p. 4). The physician maintained that Garrianna's injuries could not have resulted from walking into a door jamb, as her parents claimed, and he urged the hospital social worker to file an abuse report.

Based on its investigation, the department petitioned to remove Garrianna from her home. It was granted, and physical custody of the girl was given to the department, which was to supervise parental visits. A permanent custody hearing was initially scheduled for July 1982. However, a parallel criminal investigation had led to an assault indictment against Garrianna's father, and the custody hearing was continued by the presiding judge until after disposition of the criminal charges in Superior Court. Garrianna's parents separated, and Mrs. Quinn continued to cooperate with the social worker assigned to the case, even though she refused to admit that any abuse had occurred.

The custody hearing in December 1982 returned Garrianna to her mother but left legal custody with the Department of Human Services. Mr. Quinn was ordered to maintain a separate residence. Although the worker had doubts that Garrianna could be protected under these circumstances, she did not question the agreement, on advice of the assistant attorney general assigned to the case. In June 1983, Garrianna was returned to her mother, based on the fact that she had been well cared for and not injured since December, but the state retained legal custody. The department was asked to supervise the case an additional six months.

In August 1983, Mr. Quinn suffered a heart attack and moved back home with wife and child to convalesce. He left their home again in December, when Mrs. Quinn insisted he not move back permanently but said he could visit. In February 1984, on one of those visits, he inflicted injuries that caused Garrianna's death.

The child's death outraged the citizens of Maine, whose small population and traditions of respect for individual and family create a strong sense of community. Most of the initial concern was over the department's apparent failure to fulfill its obligation to protect children in jeopardy. However, as the public debate continued, several other issues emerged. First, the failure in the case came to be seen as that of the child welfare and legal systems to collaborate in the best interests of the child. The number of independent actors involved in the legal proceedings of Garrianna's case was sobering. The department—an executive-branch agency headed by a commissioner appointed by the governor—conducted the initial investigation. It was represented in the civil proceedings (in District Court) by an assistant attorney general assigned to the department. Meanwhile, the state police investigated the criminal charges, which were brought by a locally elected district attorney in Superior Court. Defense attorneys, acting in what they believed to be the best interests of Mr. Quinn, sought continuances in the criminal proceeding and urged their client not to cooperate in the civil investigation or to undergo treatment.

Since both the civil and criminal proceedings were part of crowded court dockets, neither judge had become well-informed on children's issues. Because of the complexity of the proceedings, the department, the assistant attorney general, and the judges all made erroneous assumptions and appeared to misstep through the jurisdictional confusion. The net effect was that neither the courts nor the department could protect Garrianna.

Before we examine the department's response to the Quinn death, it is important to understand the events immediately preceding. Joseph Brennan, elected governor of Maine in 1978, had appointed as Commissioner of Human Services Michael Petit, a strong advocate of children's issues. Early in the administration, four children, all known to the department through prior abuse or neglect investigation, had died within a six-week period. Three of the children were suspected to have died at the hands of family members. In response to the deaths, Commissioner Petit had staff investigate all child deaths in Maine between 1976 and 1980. Among their findings, two are noteworthy. First, the leading cause of child deaths in that period was disease: twice as many children died from disease as from the second leading cause, accidents (State of Maine, 1983); disease was the leading cause of death for children under five, accidents the leading cause for children over five. Second, for all causes of child death, rates for poor children were three times those for nonpoor children: poor children were 3.5 times as likely to die from disease, 4.9 times as likely to die from fire, and 5.0 times as likely to die as a result of homicide.

The department's report circulated widely across the state. The commissioner convened a statewide conference to review the findings, and, based on the conference, he assembled a task force to generate policy recommendations, which were reviewed, in turn, by a second statewide conference. One result of this prolonged discussion was the expansion of income maintenance coverage for children. While federal grants for Aid to Families with Dependent Children (AFDC) had been reduced, the Maine legislature increased state support for that program. The task force's recommendations were used to develop a special children's budget, signed into law in April 1984, which included $1 million each for prenatal care, payments to foster parents, and expansion of AFDC to serve families where the principal wage earner is unemployed.

The Response of the Department of Human Services

Against the background of the child death study, Commissioner Petit's first response to the Garrianna Quinn death was a thorough internal investigation of the case. The investigation report, which took two months and eleven drafts to prepare, stated flatly that the case represented a failure of several institutions to protect Garrianna. It concluded: "While the Department's investigation does not point to any single action which might have prevented the death of Garrianna Quinn, it does raise disturbing questions about certain criminal justice, medical, and human services practices, policies and conduct and how they interact with each other. . . . The greatest weakness is at the junction where different disciplines and systems come together to protect children" (State of Maine, 1984a, pp. 8-9).

The report described certain unsatisfactory department policies and procedures as well as departmental attempts to correct administrative failures, such as promising to develop protocols with hospitals, and establishing clearer procedures for appealing court decisions. However, the report stopped short of recommending specific changes in other agencies, merely raising issues for them to consider, such as when it mentioned that the department would initiate meetings with the Maine Bar Association to "learn if there are ways to make improvement in the law and practice of child custody proceedings" (State of Maine, 1984a, p. 16).

The commissioner's next step was to persuade the governor to convene a working group on child abuse and neglect legal proceedings, which was chaired by the commissioner, staffed by his department, and included the chief district and superior court judges, district attorneys, the commissioner of public safety, child advocates and program experts, an assistant attorney general, and department representatives. This group met for several months, at the end of which it made fifty-one recommendations on accessibility of records, child abuse reporting, court personnel, child abuse education, court procedures, court facilities, criminal penalties, treatment resources, and department administrative changes (State of Maine, 1984b).

The commissioner devoted nearly full time to promoting the

report, which was written in clear, simple English and published in attractive format. He presented the report to the governor and distributed copies to legislators, advocates, newspapers, broadcasters, and participants in local and state child welfare programs. He convened a series of public hearings across the state for local press, interested professionals, the public, and legislators, attending each hearing in order to describe the problem as well as the proposed solutions. The department prepared an omnibus bill that included nonfinancial, nonadministrative recommendations and was submitted to the legislature after the governor's review and with his full support.

While the omnibus bill was under review, other changes in the legal system occurred. The chief judge of Superior Court ordered all child abuse cases placed third on the court's docket, following homicides and legally mandated proceedings. The state police commissioner created a child abuse investigation unit by transferring resources internally. The District Attorney Association developed a common protocol for investigating child abuse cases.

The review of the omnibus bill did not occur without controversy. Opponents argued for the rights of parents and against increasing the power of the state in family life. Yet the bill passed by a comfortable margin, attributable to a strong alliance of supporters, including the executive, the courts, and key legislators as well as interested parties from around the state. Although the commissioner was among the bill's chief advocates, his clout was not the only explanation for the bill's passage. A key element in the case was the way the department cultivated political consensus through its approach to the problem and search for an answer.

The Department/Executive Role

The working group can be considered a success in Maine policy development thanks to three key actions taken by the commissioner and the department. First, the department investigated the Quinn case thoroughly and made its findings public. There is a tendency in human services to retreat from the public in a crisis, often conveniently justified as "protecting client confidentiality." As the Maine experience shows, retreat is not inevitable.

Certain names, events, and official reports must be kept confidential, but much can be made public. Commissioner Petit believed that doing so would maintain a level of public trust in the agency and was a critical first step in creating a supportive policy environment. He stated, "When presented with the facts, the public will handle the situation in a mature way. The public can understand that we are not perfect, but it does expect us to respond to a crisis" (interview with author, April 2, 1985). Contrast that with the Maine Department of Education's refusal to comment when confronted with a newspaper report of sexual abuse of students in a state school for the blind: the press, suspecting a cover-up, hounded the department for a year, intent on uncovering a story the department could have revealed itself. The lesson seems to be that when the public agency initiates the investigation and admits system errors openly, it can turn an instance of wrongdoing within the bureaucracy into an opportunity for policy change.

In the second key action, the commissioner, building on the base established by the report, assembled a well-staffed working group that brought together all the influential actors whose policies and procedures were called into question. The commissioner carefully selected the members, knew most of them, and knew all were interested in the state's response to child abuse. The judges, for example, had previously expressed concern over the rising number of cases on the dockets. The working group was deliberately convened under the auspices of the governor because the commissioner wanted the governor's visibility to lend significance to the proceedings. Based on his experience, the commissioner also believed the governor's endorsement would be critical to the enactment and implementation of the working group's recommendations. The group even met in the cabinet room, and the governor spent time with the group, including half a day listening to the recommendations. The working group's staff of key officials from the Department of Human Services, including the director of the Bureau of Social Services and a special assistant to the commissioner, ensured that requests for information were handled promptly. The presence of a legislative assistant promoted an early and continuing dialogue, at the staff level, with the legislature.

The third key action by the department and commissioner

was to promote the working group's recommendations. The department engaged in what one staff member called a saturation strategy. Special attention was devoted to preparing the report: snappy graphic design and the elimination of professional jargon made reading easier. The document's formal presentation to the governor gave it added visibility. Its focus on children's issues was made clear when it was distributed to the press, legislature, professionals, and laypersons. Public hearings were used to reinforce the findings and strengthen local support. Local hearings provided an event for press coverage and gave the commissioner a chance to stress the importance of the recommendations.

Throughout the process, the commissioner was aggressive in dealing with the press, getting to know reporters and editors and providing them with a continual flow of information. He called press conferences at key junctures, distributed documents, and communicated with editors on a regular basis, including calling editors of daily newspapers to discuss the progress of the omnibus bill.

He also consistently responded to columns, editorials, and news stories that he felt inaccurately portrayed the situation, including many articles following the Quinn death that were critical of and sometimes hostile to the department. He always expressed sorrow for the death, then described the magnitude of the task, citing the growing number of child abuse referrals and the increasing complexity of cases, and holding that the department had tried its best, but could do better. He always concluded by citing changes in policy and practices the department would seek.

For example, before the working group was to release its report, four-year-old Angela Palmer was asphyxiated in a kitchen oven by her parents. Most of the extensive press reaction was hostile to the department. One widely read columnist (Pitt, 1984) asked why the department could not prevent such deaths, criticizing the commissioner for blaming the judiciary for the Quinn death, and suggesting that the real problem was within the department. The commissioner's carefully worded response was immediate. He agreed with the general issues raised in the column, but added, "It is equally true that 140 child protective workers alone cannot possibly protect the nearly 18,000 children who will be referred to the Department of Human Services this year" (Petit, 1984). He claimed that the charges against the department were an unfair indictment of his workers, but spent most of the letter describing the way the department, the state legislature, and others could improve the system, citing the working group as a major step toward change.

This incident deserves our attention here because the Palmer death had the potential for derailing the working group's effort. Petit's response recognizing the horror of the death was carefully balanced with an invitation for the public to help solve the problem. He avoided promising that the working group's efforts would prevent all such deaths, but emphasized their recommendations as an important element of the change necessary to respond to the circumstances in the Quinn and Palmer cases. Rather than being totally defensive, he used the newspaper dialogue as an opportunity to discuss the need for legal changes.

The Importance of Information

The Quinn case and the working group clearly illustrate the importance of information as a resource in creating climates for change. Kanter (1983) calls information a source of power, and suggests that agents of change will leverage their sources of power to maximum advantage to support a desired innovation. Unfortunately, using information, particularly formal studies, in public debate is often frustrating. Carefully prepared policy statements can go unread because they do not provide policy influentials with the information they need, in a way they understand, and at a time when they need it (O'Hare, 1981). Information that supports a particular policy alternative invites controversy and can become an object of debate rather than a resource for debate (Weiss and Gruber, 1984).

The Maine experience suggests that public administrators should use information not so much to persuade others to endorse a specific proposal but to set an agenda and influence the policy environment. What the Commissioner and Department of Human Services did was employ information to define an issue and shape the public expectation that the problem would be solved. They subsequently assembled and guided a group of people who could solve the problem. These two functions—defining the issue and guiding the problem-solving process—deserve closer attention.

Defining the Issue. Too little attention has been given to using information to define issues and influence agendas. In children's issues, as in many human service areas, authority to solve problems is diffuse. In Maine, authority to deal with the Quinn case was spread among state and local agents, some of whom—judges, for example—had a tradition of independence. Focusing this group on a specific case became the key to policy development. Each was working on a separate agenda with a set of priorities arrived at independently. There was little chance that the commissioner could marshal the political influence to force or even persuade them to endorse a solution of his own choosing, no matter how well justified the policy. However, all of the actors were political officials, sensitive to public perceptions and expectations. The commissioner was able to take an instance of public outrage to focus this set of political actors on a common priority.

Perhaps the department should have pressed for consolidation of decision-making authority over children. The argument against that is two-fold. First, the diffusion of authority in the Quinn case was firmly based in the constitutional separation of powers. The tradition of independence of judges, for example, is the result of a deliberate effort to prevent consolidation of authority. Second, each of the actors involved had his or her own base of political power. Only two of the working group members had been appointed to their regular jobs by the governor; the others had been either independently elected or appointed by an independently elected official. To limit their power would require enormous legislative support.

Recognizing the diffusion of authority, the department used the publicity that followed the Quinn case to shape a public expectation that all actors would focus on a common problem. The investigation did not attempt to dictate solutions but tried to identify areas in which joint attention was needed. Critical to such an effort was presenting easily understood information. By recognizing that legislators, the press, and the public have neither the time nor inclination to plow through complex details to understand agency operations, Commissioner Petit published clear reports and took time to present the contents to various groups. The child death study, for example, included a detailed statistical analysis for interested professionals but had front material written in nonprofessional language that highlighted the major findings. Petit's press conferences and speeches focused on those major findings. None of this advocated a particular policy option, but it set the expectation that the state would do something to reduce the likelihood of death for poor children. That atmosphere enhanced the attractiveness of the AFDC budget increases subsequently proposed by the governor.

Sometimes, defining a problem leads directly to solutions. In the case of the working group, certain of the actors operated independently to change policy once they understood the problem. The chief Superior Court judge's change in the priority of child abuse cases is an example. Commissioner Petit could not have effected that change on his own and, in fact, never thought of it or suggested it. There was really no way the commissioner could have known all the available options, nor was he in a position to implement them. The leader's approach should be to define problems in ways that get the attention of the policy influentials that control the various components of a program.

Guiding Problem Solving. Much management literature is aimed at helping leaders make better decisions. The Quinn case suggests that sometimes the leader's job is not to make a decision but to manage a process through which others can make a decision or, to borrow from March and Olsen (1979), to influence the outcome of the game by tilting the field. The Maine experience suggests that this tilting function is particularly appropriate when decision-making authority is diffuse. Drucker (1967) claims that an effective decision is one that takes account of all available information and is made through a process that generates the support needed for its implementation. Acting alone, Commissioner Petit could not have met both criteria. He did not understand legal procedures fully. Nor did he have authority over the various individuals who would have to act to change legal proceedings. To make an effective decision under such circumstances requires that the actors with pertinent information and relevant authority play a prominent role in decision making. Those with information should be consulted; those with authority should have a voice in articulating options and forging recommendations.

For Petit, those with relevant information were also those with authority. The working group was thus a sound strategy, and the department took several steps to set the stage for its success. First, it included not only actors who had stature with critical constituents but people who had experience with child abuse as well. Second, it set up the group under the governor's auspices, lending priority status to the work and resulting in the governor's endorsement of the recommendations, both of which aspects encouraged the chief judges' participation and all members' full attention to the effort.

The third step the department took was to use information during deliberations. The staff's job was to answer the working group's questions as they arose. In Maine, this avoided disputes over the validity of data and premature dismissal of data or policy options.

The final step was the department's nearly tireless promotion of the working group's recommendations, including Petit's public actions in helping arrange the governor's continuing participation and his serving as a target for opponents. By distributing the report widely and scheduling public hearings to build awareness, Petit made it easier for working group members to discuss the recommendations with their colleagues. (A particularly interesting example: the chief justice of the Maine Supreme Court called Petit after the working group had begun and asked for a briefing, which probably made it easier for the judges on the working group to promote the report.)

Conclusion

Despite factors specific to the Quinn case—such as that both houses of the legislature were controlled by the governor's party, the state's relatively small population and "tight culture," the simple structure of state government, and the relationship between the commissioner and the governor—there are several lessons about creating climates for change to be learned here. First, human services leaders need to focus on the way they deal with information. The Maine experience suggests that information should be marshaled to set the stage for policy debate, not just to advance a position. It seems to say that information on specific policy options should be presented only when those who have authority to make and implement decisions are ready to use it. All public issues are not as attention-grabbing as child abuse. On the other hand, other issues may not be as hard to solve. The Maine experience suggests that whatever the issue, the leader should manage information not only to evaluate the consequences of policy alternatives or to persuade others of the wisdom of decisions already made, but to influence the policy agenda. Doing so requires evenhanded analysis, aggressive involvement of key actors in reviewing and responding to analysis, and consistent, active promotion of the information to the public, to increase both your freedom of policy choice and your chances for effective action.

Second, human services leaders must understand the distribution of policy influence and build coalitions that respect the independent power of relevant actors. There is no need to strong-arm individuals outside the human services agency or to second-guess their agendas. Better to draw them into a coalition of influential people who share a problem.

Finally, this case teaches us that leaders need to spend time and energy informing and listening to the public.

Yes, the Maine case and Michael Petit's position in Maine were unique. But any human services leader·can have a similar influence on public debate over issues critical to his or her programs. The message is clear. Leaders must marshal information to define and encourage public ownership of human services problems. They must build coalitions of influential people to help solve problems and develop new programs to meet changing needs. They must be constant allies to those people, keeping the issues on the public agenda and keeping the public informed.

11

Conclusion: The Art of Effective Leadership

After listening patiently to my enthusiastic presentation of results-oriented management, one of my colleagues observed, "If you're good at this, you'll get fired." He went on to say that people who insisted on managing for outcomes rather than for preserving the status quo made enemies, would spend irreplaceable political capital, and eventually would have to leave. If he were the one fired, my colleague mused, he was not so sure he would like results-oriented management after all.

My colleague was echoing Henry Kissinger (1979), who observed that a political leader comes into office with a fixed stock of political capital and then proceeds to spend it on an agenda. Kissinger firmly believes that the stock cannot be replenished. He maintains that the consequences of change always lead to a net reduction in the leader's power to persuade.

Though Kissinger's view may be extreme, there is a point to his warning: when managers manage for outcomes, they inevitably challenge the status quo. That's the stuff of leadership. Programs change because clients and their problems change, all of which raises concerns that can eventually inhibit the leader's flexibility.

There's plenty of anecdotal evidence that this is so. I am reminded of the struggle undertaken by the North Carolina Department of Human Resources in the late 1970s to close the Confederate Widows' Home, which then housed five women, daughters of

149

confederate soldiers, each over 90. The cost of maintaining the old facility was extraordinarily high, and yet the psychological cost they would pay to move was also high. The story made good press, and it took the department two years to move the widows into what turned out to be more comfortable quarters at lower cost. In the process, several managers nearly lost their job by underestimating the resistance to change.

In government, it is no secret why those who manage for outcomes generate opposition: outspoken on behalf of new programs and clients, they will try to shift resources away from sacred cows and to innovative services. This has at least three risks. First, since such activist executives are often those most closely associated with an outgoing chief executive, they risk being canned after the change in administrations.

The leader also risks burning out. Taking difficult stands is hard work, and it is emotionally draining. I know of one state executive who, having served a governor of a party different from his own, declined when asked by both gubernatorial candidates to remain on the job. He had been responsible for imposing a cap on nursing home rates in his state, and although that helped contain Medicare costs, the industry's powerful friends could not have overturned the limit but also could have made the official's life miserable.

Of course, as an organization changes, the activist's cause may lose priority. The department that needed an activist last year may this year need a systems manager to institutionalize the ideas the activist championed. Program emphasis can shift from one client group to another, making it appropriate to bring in a leader with a somewhat different background. Organizations may progress through a life cycle, from birth, when new programs are created, to maturity, when they have become institutionalized, to decline, when they are past their prime and need to change. Herbert Kaufman (1976) has found that to be true in the federal government; it is probably true at the state and local levels as well.

Although I seem to be arguing that leaders must know when to leave an organization, must know when their skills are no longer appropriate for the organization, the political environment, or the programs and clients, there are many examples of leaders who remain at the same organization for a long time, such as Jack Dempsey in Michigan and Merle Springer in Texas. Dempsey directed Social Services for nineteen years, achieving national recognition as a leader in the field. Springer served as executive deputy of Human Services in Texas for many years. True, in Dempsey's case there was remarkable political continuity for much of his tenure, and Springer's department has been partially shielded from political controversy through a commission structure. But the fact is that some leaders survive.

Is There Security in Leadership?

Even though there is no job security for human services leaders, there is great security in leadership. Most leaders are what William James (1902) would call a twice-born personality type: having had a rough time of life, having had to struggle to survive, they have learned how to stand apart. They do not derive their sense of self from being accepted by their environments, but instead measure themselves by their own standards.

Bennis and Nanus (1985) help us understand exactly what the leader's standards are. Their study of leaders shows that leaders consistently have two characteristics: They have high self-regard, and they are outcome driven. Leaders know their strengths and weaknesses and are able to build relationships with others that complement their strengths and compensate for their weaknesses. Bennis and Nanus, in describing positive self-regard as the product of emotional wisdom, avoid using the word *maturity*. They say (p. 65), "our leaders seemed to retain many of the positive characteristics of a child: enthusiasm for people, spontaneity, imagination, and an unlimited capacity to learn new behaviors."

Emotional wisdom is the capacity to relate positively with other people. Bennis and Nanus found five skills characteristic of their leaders' positive relationships. First, leaders accept people for what they are, instead of trying to make them into what they would like them to be. Second, they deal with the present, evaluating people in terms of their current capacity, not their past mistakes. Third, they treat close associates with unfailing courtesy. Fourth, they trust others. Fifth, they are able to work without continual approval and recognition from others.

Effective leaders, in this view, understand themselves and relate to others in a realistic, dignified, friendly way. In other words, they have high self-regard. Without going further into the psychology of leadership, it is enough to point out here that without self-regard—the product of thorough self-knowledge and an openness to working with people—the leader who follows the advice in this book will be less effective than she or he might be. This book does not supplant the need for sensitivity to self and others, it complements it.

Bennis and Nanus also say that leaders are driven by outcomes, not process. That is where this book can help. Bennis and Nanus find that successful leaders are excited by the prospects of making things happen. With results-oriented management, you can be excited about making things happen in human services.

High self-regard and a focus on outcomes will make you a successful leader, but that still does not ensure you keep your job. Leaders accept that because, as William James observed, they rest on an altogether different source of security, the knowledge of what they can do, what they have done, and the difference that makes. That may not be the kind of security that pays the mortgage or gets the kids through school, but it does give leaders the strength to lead. States, localities, and voluntary agencies across the country are crying for leadership.

Beliefs and Values

Thomas Watson, Jr., retired chief executive of IBM, helped make IBM the world's largest computer company. Watson has admitted he was no computer expert. How, then, could he have built such a successful high-technology firm? Watson, in *Business and Its Beliefs* (1963), says that what he did was to give the people at IBM something to believe in. He mildly criticizes his colleagues in professional management for their reluctance to discuss beliefs and values, because, he maintains, shared values are the foundation of a strong organization. Such a foundation, he says, must be comprised of three important beliefs for the organization to be successful.

First, the people in the organization must believe their clients or customers are important. How can you give full effort to serving other people who you do not believe matter? Watson urged IBM executives to stress the importance of their customers. Every IBM executive, including Watson, called on customers during the year. In words and action the message was clear: the customer is the boss.

Second, employees must feel that they matter. Watson insisted that every employee be called by a title—Mr., Mrs., or Miss—not for reasons of formality, but so no employee would feel like a second-class citizen. Now everyone at IBM goes by first names, for the same reason. IBM is widely recognized for the high standards to which its employees are held and for the training, attention, and rewards lavished on them. The continual message within the organization is that people matter.

But, only with the third belief—that the work itself makes a difference in the world—will believing that clients and employees matter lead to success.

Watson's beliefs about leadership are remarkably close to the ideas of Victor Frankel, a survivor of Mauthausen, the Austrian death camp, and previously a prominent Viennese psychiatrist and student of Freud. Frankel published his observations of his fellow prisoners in the book *Man's Search for Meaning* (1963). Among those prisoners were individuals who had the strongest sense of purpose and desire to live of any human beings he had ever met. Those brave prisoners, Frankel observes, defined their sense of purpose in terms of what they could do for others, not in terms of their own needs. If Watson and Frankel are right, and I believe they are, then results-oriented management makes even more sense, because it is a systematic way for leaders to focus themselves and their organizations on clients. It organizes information, plans, goals, and resources so every individual in an agency can clearly see how to improve the quality of life for others. It brings dignity to human services because it conveys dignity to clients.

It is sobering to measure many human services organizations against Watson's three beliefs. Our clients are often the subject of patronizing references in public, in the press, and even among our staffs. They are stigmatized and spoken of in pejorative terms. Our employees, who work in crowded quarters and are all too often poorly paid and poorly trained, have to handle large caseloads under intense time pressure. We are so busy solving problems and responding to crises that we seldom note the true contribution our work makes to individuals, families, and communities.

While results-oriented management cannot change all of that, it can change a lot. It is not magic—it cannot remove the constraints on your ability to reward performance or shift resources—but consider what it does do. It places clients at the forefront of your planning. It defines agency activity in terms of clients, sending a powerful message to the organization about the importance of clients. It provides employees with clear goals that are directly related to the agency's overall expectations. It helps focus training and available rewards on achieving those client-centered goals, thereby enhancing employee self-worth. It provides direct, continuing evidence of agency impact on the lives of others. It shows how daily and annual achievement of objectives leads to greater dignity for clients and their communities.

Thomas Watson may have had a lot more advantages as a leader than we do. He had more authority over his organization, more money to spend, more flexibility in designing his management systems. But in one major respect, human services has a distinct advantage over IBM. The work we do leads directly to better lives for others. Human services is the heart of our collective attempt to build a decent, fair, and humane society. I hope this book helps you exploit that advantage so you can continue leading this important effort.

References

Adler, M. *A Vision for the Future.* New York: Macmillan, 1984.

Allison, G. *Essence of Decision.* Boston: Little, Brown, 1970.

Ambrose, S. *Eisenhower, The President.* New York: Simon & Schuster, 1984.

Anderson, S., and Ball, S. *The Profession and Practice of Program Evaluation.* San Francisco: Jossey-Bass, 1978.

Andrews, K. *The Concept of Corporate Strategy.* Homewood, Ill.: Dow Jones-Irwin, 1971.

Ansoff, I. *Corporate Strategy.* New York: McGraw-Hill, 1965.

Ansoff, I. *Strategic Management.* New York: Wiley, 1979.

Anthony, R., Dearden, J., and Vancil, R. *Management Control Systems.* Homewood, Ill.: Irwin, 1972.

Anthony, R., and Young, D. *Management Control in Nonprofit Organizations.* Homewood, Ill.: Irwin, 1984.

Argyris, C. *Executive Leadership.* New York: Harper & Row, 1953.

Attkisson, C., Hargreaves, W., Horowitz, W., and Sorenson, J. (eds.). *Evaluation of Human Service Programs.* New York: Academic Press, 1978.

Bardach, E. *The Skill Factor in Politics.* Berkeley: University of California Press, 1972.

Bardach, E. *The Implementation Game.* Cambridge, Mass.: MIT Press, 1977.

Bardach, E. "The Political Entrepreneur Amidst the Flux." Paper presented to the Association for Public Policy Analysis and Management, October, 1987.

Behn, B. "The State of Knowledge about Public Management." Paper delivered at the Annual Research Conference of the Association for Public Policy Analysis and Management, Austin, Tex., November 1, 1986.

Behn, B. "Getting from Here to There: Management by Groping Along." Paper presented to the Association for Public Policy Analysis and Management, October 1987a.

Behn, B. "Managing Innovation in Welfare, Training and Work: Some Lessons from ET Choices in Massachusetts." Paper presented to the American Political Science Association, September 1987b.

Behrman, J. "Can Managers Be Leaders?" In *Essays in Business Ethics*, unpublished manuscript, Chapel Hill, N.C., 1986.

Bell, D. *The Coming of the Post-Industrial Society*. New York: Basic Books, 1976.

Bennis, W., and Nanus, B. *Leaders*. New York: Harper & Row, 1985.

Blanchard, K., Zigarmi, D., and Zigarmi, P. *Leadership and the One-Minute Manager*. New York: Morrow, 1985.

Burgelman, R., and Sayles, L. *Inside Corporate Innovation*. New York: Free Press, 1986.

Burns, J. *Leadership*. New York: Harper & Row, 1978.

Campbell, D., and Stanley, J. *Experimental and Quasi-Experimental Designs for Research*. Chicago: Rand McNally, 1966.

Carter, R. *The Accountable Agency*. Beverly Hills, Calif.: Sage, 1983.

Center for the Study of Social Policy. "Preserving Families in Crisis: Financial and Political Options." Unpublished paper, Washington, D.C., 1986.

Clemens, J., and Mayer, D. *The Classic Touch: Lessons in Leadership from Homer to Hemingway*. Homewood, Ill.: Irwin, 1987.

Cook, T., and Campbell, D. *Quasi-Experimentation: Design and Analysis Issues for Field Settings*. Chicago: Rand McNally, 1979.

Craft, J., Epley, S., and Theison, W. *Child Welfare Forecasting*. Springfield, Ill.: Thomas, 1980.

Daniel, R. "Management Information Crisis." *Harvard Business Review,* 1961, *39* (5), 108-118.

Derthick, M. *The Influence of Federal Grants.* Cambridge, Mass.: Harvard University Press, 1970.

Derthick, M. *Policymaking for Social Security.* Washington, D.C.: Brookings Institution, 1979.

Doig, J., and Hargrove, E. *Leadership and Innovation.* Baltimore: Johns Hopkins Press, 1987.

Drucker, P. "The Effective Decision." *Harvard Business Review,* 1967, *45* (1), 92-98.

Drucker, P. *Managing in Turbulent Times.* New York: Harper and Row, 1980.

Frankel, V. *Man's Search for Meaning.* New York: Pocket Books, 1963.

Graham, O. "Uses and Misuses of History: Roles in Policymaking." *The Public Historian,* 1983, *5* (2), 5-19.

Graham, O. "Uses and Misuses of History in the Debate over Immigration Reform." *The Public Historian,* 1986, *8* (2), 41-64.

Hatry, H., Blair, L., Fisk, D., and Kimmel, W. *Program Analysis for State and Local Governments.* Washington, D.C.: Urban Institute, 1976.

Hatry, H., Winnie, R., and Fisk, D. *Practical Program Evaluation for State and Local Government.* Washington, D.C.: Urban Institute, 1981.

Henderson, B. "The Product Portfolio." In *Perspectives.* (ed.) Boston: Boston Consulting Group, 1970.

Hersey, P. *The Situational Leader.* New York: Warner Books, 1984.

Hersey, P., and Blanchard, K. *Management of Organization Behavior.* Englewood Cliffs, N.J.: Prentice-Hall, 1982.

Iacocca, L. *Iacocca: An Autobiography.* New York: Bantam Books, 1984.

James, W. *The Varieties of Religious Experience.* New York: Longmans, Green, 1902.

Kanter, R. *The Change Masters.* New York: Simon & Schuster, 1983.

Kaufman, H. *Are Government Organizations Immortal?* Washington, D.C.: Brookings Institution, 1976.

Kaufman, H. *Red Tape.* Washington, D.C.: Brookings Institution, 1977.

Keeney, R., and Raiffa, H. *Decisions with Multiple Objectives: Preference and Value Trade-Offs.* New York: Wiley, 1976.

Kissinger, H. *The White House Years.* Boston: Little, Brown, 1979.

Koss, M., and others. *Social Services: What Happens to the Clients?* Washington, D.C.: Urban Institute, 1979.

Leman, C. "Gordon Chase at the Health Services Administration: Lessons from a Successful Public Manager." Paper presented to the Association for Public Policy Analysis and Public Management, October, 1987.

Levin, R. *The Executive's Illustrated Primer of Long-Range Planning.* Englewood Cliffs, N.J.: Prentice-Hall, 1981.

Lynn, L. *The State and Human Services.* Cambridge, Mass.: MIT Press, 1980.

Lynn, L. *Minding the Public's Business: The Job of the Government Executive.* New York: Basic Books, 1981.

March, J., and Olsen, J. *Ambiguity and Choice in Organizations.* Bergen, Norway: Universitats Forlagest, 1979.

Mintzberg, H. *The Structuring of Organizations.* Englewood Cliffs, N.J.: Prentice-Hall, 1979.

Mishan, E. *Cost Benefit Analysis.* New York: Praeger, 1976.

National Academy of Public Administration. *Reorganization in Florida.* Washington, D.C.: The Academy, 1977.

National Academy of Public Administration. *After a Decade.* Washington, D.C.: The Academy, 1986.

Neustadt, R. *Presidential Power.* New York: Wiley, 1980.

Neustadt, R., and May, E. *Thinking in Time.* New York: Free Press, 1986.

O'Hare, M. "Information Management and Public Choice." In J. Crecine (ed.), *Research in Public Policy Analysis and Management.* Vol. 1. Greenwich, Conn.: JAI Press, 1981.

Peters, T. "Symbols, Patterns and Settings: The Optimistic Case for Getting Things Done." *Organization Dynamics,* 1978, 7, 3-23.

Peters, T., and Waterman, R. *In Search of Excellence.* New York: Harper & Row, 1982.

Petit, M. Letter to the Editor, *Portland Sunday Telegram,* November 6, 1984.

Pitt, G. "Who Killed Angela Palmer?" *Portland Sunday Telegram,* November 6, 1984.

Porter, M. *Competitive Strategy: Techniques for Analyzing Industries and Competitors.* New York: Free Press, 1980.

Porter, M. *Competitive Advantage Creating and Sustaining Superior Performance.* New York: Free Press, 1985.

Pressman, J., and Wildavsky, A. *Implementation.* Berkeley: University of California Press, 1973.

Raiffa, H. *Decision Analysis.* Reading, Mass.: Addison-Wesley, 1968.

Rockart, J. "Chief Executives Define Their Own Data Needs." *Harvard Business Review,* 1979, *57* (2), 81–91.

Saleznick, A. "Managers and Leaders: Are They Different?" *Harvard Business Review,* 1977, *55* (3), 67–78.

Sayles, L. *Leadership.* New York: McGraw-Hill, 1979.

Schainblatt, A. *Monitoring the Outcomes of State Mental Health Treatment Programs.* Washington, D.C.: Urban Institute, 1977.

Schainblatt, A., and Hatry, H. *Mental Health Services: What Happens to the Client?* Washington, D.C.: Urban Institute, 1979.

State of Maine, Department of Human Services. *Children's Deaths in Maine.* Augusta, Me.: State of Maine, Department of Human Resources, 1983.

State of Maine, Department of Human Services. "Child Protective Report on the Death of Garrianna Quinn." Augusta, Me.: State of Maine, Department of Human Resources, April 9, 1984a.

State of Maine, Department of Human Services. *Protecting Our Children: Not Without Changes in the Legal System.* Report of the Governor's Working Group on Child Abuse and Neglect, Legal Proceedings. Augusta, Me.: State of Maine, Department of Human Resources, 1984b.

Steiner, G. *Top Management Planning.* London: Collier-Macmillan, 1969.

Steiner, G. *Strategic Planning.* London: Collier-Macmillan, 1979.

Theobold, W. *The Evaluation of Human Service Programs.* Champaign, Ill.: Management Learning Labs, 1985.

Thompson, M. *Benefit Cost Analysis for Program Evaluation.* Beverly Hills, Calif.: Sage, 1980.

Tregoe, B., and Zimmerman, J. *Top Management Strategy.* New York: Simon & Schuster, 1980.

Watson, T. *Business and Its Beliefs.* New York: McGraw-Hill, 1963.

Weick, K. *The Social Psychology of Organization*. Reading, Mass.: Addison-Wesley, 1969.

Weiss, C. Evaluation Research: *Methods of Assessing Program Effectiveness*. Englewood Cliffs, N.J.: Prentice-Hall, 1972.

Weiss, J., and Gruber, J. "Use of Knowledge for Control in Fragmented Policy Areas." *Journal of Public Policy Analysis and Management*, 1984, *3* (2), 223–256.

Wildavsky, A. *The Politics of the Budgetary Process*. Boston: Little, Brown, 1974.

Index